AGAINST ALL ODDS

A VENTURE OF FAITH WITH THE HILL TRIBES OF BANGLADESH

JAY WALSH

Association of Baptists for World Evangelism
P.O. Box 8585
Harrisburg, PA 17105-8585
(717) 774-7000

ABWE Canada
160 Adelaide St. South, Suite 205
London, Ontario N5Z 3L1
(519) 690-1009

 PUBLISHING®

Except where otherwise indicated, all Scripture
quotations in this book are taken from the Holy
Bible, King James Version, 1611.

AGAINST ALL ODDS
Copyright © 1995 by ABWE Publishing
Harrisburg, Pennsylvania 17105

Library of Congress Cataloging-in-Publication Data

Walsh, D. Jay, 1932–
    Against All Odds: A venture of faith with the
        hill tribes of Bangladesh/Jay Walsh
    Autobiographical, Non-fiction
    ISBN 1-888796-00-6 (Trade Paper)

Printed in the United States of America.

DEDICATION

To Eleanor,
my wife and my love who journeyed
through these pages with me.

And to our children,
God's gracious and precious gifts.

Douglas Jay Walsh
Linda Marie Zylstra
Debra Joy Collins
Phillip Martin Walsh
Sheryl Ann Petrovich
Shelley Lou Barker
Diane Janine Ford

ACKNOWLEDGEMENTS

Writing AGAINST ALL ODDS was a special experience which brought back many wonderful memories and some tears. During this process, I was blessed to have the support of my wife and family, and the help of my missionary colleagues and friends. To them I express my sincerest thanks.

To the **Publicity Committee of the Bangladesh Field Council** for their insightful comments, and, most of all, for their encouragement to complete the project.

To my fellow missionaries **Reid Minich, Mary Lou Brownell,** and **Carol Stagg**, beloved co-laborers in the gospel, whose observations, suggestions, and corrections were invaluable for completing the final manuscript.

To **Dr. Harold Amstutz** and **Mrs. Jeanette Lockerbie Johnston**, both published authors, for their encouragement to publish these stories. Dr. Amstutz said, "I hope you will pursue the project to its completion. It's worthy of every effort." Mrs. Johnston commented, "I have been both informed in depth, and blessed in my soul at the recounting of God's provision for, and His direction of you and Eleanor, as you pioneered for Him in that far-off area of the world."

To **Dr. Ernajean Lockerbie** (just Jeannie to me), who was not only a co-laborer with us for over thirty years in Bangladesh, but my editor. Her talent and creativity helped shape the book into its final form.

To my publisher, the **Association of Baptists for World Evangelism, Inc.** (ABWE), under whose auspices we have been serving since 1958.

Finally, to the dozens of people, both co-laborers and nationals, whose personal stories were included in this book, and without whom it could not have been written.

Jay Walsh

FOREWORD

Throughout our years in Bangladesh it has been Eleanor's and my joy and privilege to work with a number of colleagues who were also involved, to one degree or another, with tribal evangelism. In no way do we wish to usurp undue credit for what has happened in the tribes. We are well aware that it is the Lord who keeps the records. Unworthy servants, we humbly count it a great privilege to have shared in the action.

A book like this, which is autobiographical in nature, is not intended to be a detailed history of the tribal work in Bangladesh. To do that justice would take several volumes. Instead, I have tried to capture experiences as I remember them, especially those in which my wife and I were directly involved.

Jay Walsh

CONTENTS

CHAPTER 1

ON THE SEA
OF OBEDIENCE

*"Now the Lord had said unto Abram, get thee
out of thy country, and from thy kindred, and
from thy father's house, unto a land that I will
show thee."*

Genesis 12:1–2

Dark, cloudy skies added more gloom to an already tense situation. A monsoon rain drenched us as we sloshed across the rice paddies to the military headquarters in Lama, a government outpost and bazaar one mile west of ABWE's mission station called Hebron. Why had I been so unceremoniously summoned? And why was it necessary to be marched off between two surly looking, armed soldiers?

My wife, Eleanor, stood helplessly in the doorway as I was led away. We both wondered what would become of me and how I had gotten myself into this dilemma. Had our decision to become missionaries in East Pakistan (now Bangladesh) been a mistake? Yet we had felt confident of God's call as we bade farewell to family and friends on January 29, 1960.

Our departure will be etched forever in our memories. Eleanor and I and our three children boarded a Greek freighter bound for the distant port of Chittagong, East Pakistan. The *Hellenic Splendor*, a sleek new cargo ship, was on its maiden voyage.

Accommodations for our family were cramped but adequate. Best of all, as we would appreciate later on the voyage, the cabins were air-conditioned.

Our sixteen barrels and four crates of personal and household effects were safely stashed away in the bowels of the ship. That gave us a feeling of security as we faced an unknown and uncertain future. Our decision to go to East Pakistan was a big step of faith, but we felt comfortable and secure in the will of a loving and caring Savior who not only commissioned His disciples to evangelize the world, but also promised to go with them. The future was in His hands and we were excited to be on our way.

Departure is difficult for any missionary. Ties must be cut with parents, relatives and country. We had already done this and now our ship, moored at pier 44 in Brooklyn, New York, began to shudder under the power of its massive diesel engines. The captain barked out orders to his crew as we glided calmly into New York Harbor, past the Statue of Liberty, and out into the churning Atlantic Ocean. On that cold, sleety January night, we stood quietly on the ship's bridge and watched the New York skyline disappear into a black horizon. We were leaving our beloved America, bound for another land where God was leading us.

I was 27 years old, Eleanor 26, and our children were Douglas, 5, Linda, 3, and Debra, 1, when we started our first missionary journey. To complicate matters, we were expecting our fourth child shortly after arrival in East Pakistan. Our little family joined nine other passengers on board the *Hellenic Splendor*. That made fourteen people, not including the ship's Greek captain and crew, but no doctor. For more than fourteen passengers, maritime law required a qualified medical doctor be on board. So, as the First Mate explained, freighter companies tried to avoid that extra expense.

Shortly into the voyage that terrible malady called seasickness struck with a vengeance. My untried stomach became a victim of the pitiless sea which tossed our steel freighter like a toothpick.

One moment the ship's bow aimed up at the heavens; moments later it plunged into a watery crater. That first evening's spaghetti dinner, well lubricated in olive oil, stayed down only a couple of minutes! But a week later, well into our transatlantic crossing, I finally found my sea legs and began to really enjoy the trip.

Meeting the other passengers helped to combat the loneliness we felt after leaving our families and friends in America. Eleanor and I always enjoyed being around new people. Moreover, as the only born-again Christians aboard, we would have opportunities to witness for our Lord. After all, that was why we were going overseas.

Passenger "George Smith" was an Indian seaman being deported for illegally entering the USA. We were never able to learn his real identity, although he did share his pathetic story. Nine years earlier, he had jumped ship in Los Angeles harbor as many seamen before him had done in their desire to strike it rich in America. Having successfully avoided the U.S. Immigration authorities, he hitchhiked across the country, escaping into the underworld ghettos of the East Coast—first New York City, then Newark, and finally Philadelphia. After paying hefty fees to his criminal underworld contacts, George obtained false identification papers, including a driver's license and credit cards. That's when he became Mr. George Smith and later secured employment as a welder in a Philadelphia slum.

In Philadelphia, George found a live-in girl friend who had a daughter by a previous marriage. He grew to love this lady and was especially proud of her little girl. After nine years of cohabitation, they decided to solemnize their marriage legally. The wedding date was only a week away when, as George put it, "My luck ran out."

George had come to feel secure with a home, a car, and a welder's job. But his dream ended that week in a sleazy bar. Intoxicated and argumentative, he fought with a crony who later reported him to U.S. Immigration officials. George was arrested and, after several months in detention, was now being deported back to India. His "American dream" had ended in a nightmare. Had he married earlier, he could have qualified for American citizenship. Instead, he now faced a bleak and uncertain future.

Sometimes on the journey we thought George might commit suicide. He remained intoxicated much of the time, sulking as he gazed blankly at the restless sea. Then one day as the ship approached the Indian coastline, in a fit of anger, he shredded his deportation documents and tossed them into the ocean. We watched in disbelief.

George bade us farewell in the port of Bombay, India. We were saddened to see him leave after having spent a month with us, listening intently to the Sunday Bible messages. As Indian immigration officials marched him away, he waved back and shouted, "I WILL return to Ameerika!" Two years later we received a letter from George posted from Assam, India. He was still dreaming.

Also on board was an Indian family returning to their home in New Delhi. We shall never forget their 12-year-old daughter. One day, well into the trans-Atlantic crossing, Reeta burst into our cabin with our baby daughter in her arms. Out of breath and pale with fright, she told us that she had found Debbie wandering alone on the ship's slippery deck—near where only three drooping ropes stood between her and the surging sea!

We have never determined how a one-and-a-half-year-old baby managed to exit the cabin area, secured by heavy steel doors. And we still shudder when we think about it! The full meaning of Matthew 28:20 became an integral part of our lives that day. We realized anew that there could never be a "GO" without the "LO." Jesus not only sent his disciples, He also promised to accompany them when he announced to his followers, "Lo, I am with you." Indeed, He had boarded the *Hellenic Splendor* with us.

Another passenger was Irving, a Jewish businessman from Lexington, Kentucky. Portly and a heavy drinker, he jabbered constantly. His journey was a pleasure trip which, we learned later, turned into a shopping spree. In the port of Athens, Greece, where the ship anchored for several days for the crew to contact relatives, Irving ate food that didn't agree with him and he had stomach problems for the rest of the trip—a genuine case of the infamous "crabapple two-step" (or, to the uninitiated, diarrhea). Reduced to about two-thirds of his original waist size, Irving found it difficult to wear the wardrobe he had with him. That, however, didn't hinder him from purchasing curios, *objets d'art*, and furniture which filled his stateroom and spilled out into the ship's passageways. He would, as he often bragged to us, eventually resell these in his Lexington furniture store. For a hefty profit, of course!

Mr. and Mrs. Blood, a wealthy retired couple from south Florida, completed the passenger list. They were taking a pleasure trip to the Far East, something they had done on previous occasions. We got to know them best of all. In fact, Mrs. Blood encouraged me to conduct Sunday services during our nearly seven weeks on board ship. I was pleased for that opportunity but, after hearing my brand of Christianity, she began feeling uncomfortable. Though appearing to be religious, she obviously was not a born-again Christian, and proud of it. That was a doctrine she felt belonged to people with an inferior education.

Mr. Blood was a tall, bespectacled man, reserved and henpecked. He seldom engaged in a meaningful conversation but occasionally raised his eyes from a book to glance at us over the top of his reading glasses. In contrast, his sophisticated wife was outgoing, outspoken, and militant in her opinions. Often she raised a religious question about which she sought my opinion. Invariably, she disagreed with me.

We remember Mrs. Blood best for the time she volunteered her "humble opinion" about our decision to become foreign missionaries. She chided us soundly about the folly of our going to that "God-forsaken country" of East Pakistan. She reasoned that "the natives had their own religion" and didn't need our help. Besides, we were taking our small children to "die" there. At that point she raised her bony finger and blurted, "If you take those beautiful children to live in that filthy place, you'll be guilty of murder!" And she meant every word. Though taken aback by her bluntness, we did appreciate her compliment that our children were "beautiful."

Our exposure to Mr. and Mrs. Blood inspired me to compose the following poem:

THE BLIND

How blind the blind that will not see,
    How dark the veil is cast.
Upon their hearts no light has shone,
    That darkness is so vast.
But yet these blind go on their way,
    Deluded by this spell,
And think themselves secure and fine,
    While moving on to hell.
They think the Christians very strange,
    And scorn their narrow stand.
While they profess by that same Name
    A hope of their Fair Land.
These blind carouse and play the world,
    Yet have religious glow,
They move about with any crowd,
    And let both faces show.
But legion will their number be,
    Who stand before His Throne,
To hear His verdict on them clear,
    And with the chaff be blown.
No hope for them who spurn His blood,
    Who shun the Narrow Way,
Unless to Christ they give their souls,
    And that without delay.
Dear friend, if you are of these blind,
    With sin upon your soul,

Pray now to Him with contrite heart,
    And He will make you whole.
His light will make your blind eyes see
    The secrets of His love.
And with great joy your heart will yearn
    For treasures up above.
Then you will cast your lot with those
    Whose way you used to scorn,
And then with them onward go
    Still other blind to warn.

Forty-seven days after our departure from Brooklyn, the *Hellenic Splendor* docked in the port city of Chittagong. The Bloods obtained shore passes and left the ship to sightsee. We had to stay behind to complete immigration formalities. But even before immigration officials cleared us to disembark, the Bloods returned in a huff. They marched right past us to their stateroom without a word. Within minutes Mrs. Blood emerged with an armful of soiled towels which she heaped on the floor for laundry service. Repulsed by what they had seen, they had—literally—removed the dust of Chittagong's streets from their shoes with the ship's expensive white towels.

Eleanor and I have often remembered the Bloods and thought how gratifying it would be to meet them again and tell them that the children on board the *Hellenic Splendor* in 1960 are now grown, married, and serving the Lord—two of them, along with their spouses, as foreign missionaries.

Our memorable sea journey ended on March 17, 1960, when we disembarked in the port city of Chittagong, East Pakistan. That unforgettable chapter in our lives—the seasickness, the interesting passengers, and the Greek cuisine—was over and a new chapter was about to begin. The real beginning of our missionary careers, however, started years before, when we first came to know and love the Lord Jesus Christ.

CHAPTER 2

A HOUSE CALL PAYS OFF

"So then faith cometh by hearing, and hearing by the word of God."

Romans 10:17

After graduating from Newberry High School in 1950, I left the Upper Peninsula of Michigan to work on a farm in southern Michigan.

In those days, for young people of my family's meager financial means, high school was the pinnacle of education. College was for the "rich" kids who lived in town, whose parents owned the businesses along Main Street. They were the privileged; we, the peasants. I was eighteen years old, healthy and with a bountiful zest for life. There was a world out there for me to conquer, even though the odds might be against me. I would work hard and make my own way in life.

We were a poor, unchurched family of six living in a one-room log cabin near Newberry, Michigan, halfway between the shores of Lake Superior and Lake Michigan. That humble abode, only fourteen feet wide and sixteen feet long, provided shelter for our family until I graduated from high school. The toilet, a two-seater, stood alone in the nearby woods. A flowing well provided us with cool, clear water.

What an exciting day for me in 1950 when electricity finally reached our home! I was selected as the very first person in the family to pull the string on the lone bulb hanging in the center of the room. The days of kerosene lamps were gone! Then came the telephone. Our ring was one long and two shorts.

In the early days of my childhood, the only religious influence I remember was an occasional Sunday school class taught by Mrs. Fred Taylor in the living room of her farm home, a two-mile walk from our cabin. That faithful, godly lady, whose hands were crippled with arthritis, would thump out a hymn or two on an old piano before teaching a Bible story. One of her favorite hymns, "When He Cometh," will go with me to the grave:

> When He cometh, when He cometh,
>   To make up His jewels,
> All His jewels, precious jewels,
>   His loved and His own:
> Like the stars of the morning,
>   His bright crown adorning,
> They shall shine in their beauty,
>   Bright gems for His crown.

That song, more than any other, made me realize that Jesus loved little children and He loved even me.

My dear mother, though not a Christian at that time, provided some spiritual influence in my young life. She taught her four children a prayer which I used many times, especially when I was troubled:

> Now I lay me down to sleep,
>   I pray the Lord, my soul to keep.
> If I should die before I wake,
>   I pray Thee, Lord, my soul to take.

After sincerely praying those words I would then utter my pressing concerns and always end my prayer with, "God bless Daddy and Mommy and all the rest. And, dear Jesus, help me go to sleep tonight so I won't hear Daddy if he comes home drunk. Amen." In those early years before Dad's life was changed by the influence of the gospel, he, like many other woodsmen, pushed back the pressures of life with a few drinks at the country tavern.

Things began to change in my family, and especially in my life, the day a stranger knocked at our log cabin. My tiny mother, quickly brushing back disheveled hair, opened the door to reveal a tall, bespectacled man with a smile on his face and a Bible tucked under his arm. He introduced himself as Rev. Arthur Glen, President of the Hiawathaland Independent Baptist Mission. After some friendly talk he told us that his mission was starting a church in our community. Services would be held in a cottage on Big Manistique Lake, only three miles away.

"Would you be interested in letting your children attend our Sunday school?" he asked my mom. "We'd love to have them come."

Mother, always easy to persuade, agreed. He told her, "Next Sunday our resident missionaries, Ralph and Mabel Hill, will drive by at 9:30 a.m. to pick up the kids." With that, he thanked her and left. That simple encounter would eventually change the direction of life for each member of my family.

As promised, the following Sunday Hiawathaland missionaries Ralph and Mabel Hill stopped at our cabin and sounded their horn. They were driving a 1936 Chevrolet sedan and pulling a two-wheel trailer filled with straw. My brother, two sisters and I bolted from the house and joined the other noisy kids in the straw. That had to be the literal "grass roots" of today's bus ministry!

At twelve years of age I was duly impressed with Mr. Hill's preaching. We called him "Mr." Hill because he once told us that there was only one Reverend, and He was in Heaven. Mr. Hill's preaching centered on the message of the cross and the second coming of Christ. Both his preaching and singing reflected those wonderful biblical doctrines. One of his favorite texts was 1 Corinthians 1:18:

"For the preaching of the cross is to them that perish foolishness; but unto us who are saved it is the power of God."

He also taught us hymns about the cross of Christ. "There Is A Fountain Filled With Blood" and "The Way Of The Cross Leads Home" are two that were permanently engraved in my tender mind. Even today, a half century later, I often find myself humming those inspiring tunes. Because of Mr. Hill's faithfulness to the Great Commission of Matthew 28:16-20, numerous people in that small community turned from their selfish and wayward lives to love and serve the living God. That happened in my family, too.

Under Mr. Hill's preaching, I was greatly convicted, worrying at night that the Lord would come and I wouldn't be ready. The words of a chorus we had learned in Sunday school plagued me:

> Two shall be together, grinding at the mill,
>> Two shall be together, sleeping calm and still,
> One shall be taken and the other left behind.
>> Will you be ready when Jesus comes?

At night, lying in my bunk, I would reason with myself, *Jesus didn't come today. Maybe He won't come tomorrow.* Then followed the frightening thought, *But what if He comes tonight and I'm not ready?*

I was afraid and miserable until Christ lifted my burden at the closing ceremony of a Daily Vacation Bible School held in the two-room schoolhouse near my home. Rev. John Heykoop of Ezel, Kentucky, a dedicated man of God with a burden for winning children to Christ, conducted the DVBS that summer of 1944. He closed the program with a straightforward invitation: "If you are here tonight without Jesus but would like to be saved and live for Him, please come forward and stand with me."

I sat restlessly at the back of the room beside my younger brother, Martin, under deep conviction. As the Spirit of God spoke to my heart, I rose and started for the front, stopping momentarily to motion for my brother to join me. We two stood there facing the audience. I was only a young boy, but the peace of God filled my

life that night. I knew I was saved, something I have never doubt-
ed since. I was His and He was mine!

Many years later, when I was home on vacation from seminary,
I observed my brother on his knees in prayer. Curious about his
personal spiritual experience, I asked him when he trusted the
Lord for salvation. Smiling, he replied, "Don't you remember the
DVBS program when you motioned for me to join you? That's
when I was saved."

I often reflect on the events that led to my conversion and
thank God for intervening in my life. Where would I be today if
some cult leader, instead of Rev. Arthur Glen, had called on my
humble home in those early years? I have often pondered if, when
he called that day, did he do so with the faith to believe that a poor
family, and especially this young ruffian, could one day be a part of
Christ's Kingdom? And did he see in that young lad, standing
there behind his mother, the makings of a future missionary?

Years later, Rev. Glen spoke in our seminary chapel. He started
his message by saying, "I really don't feel worthy to stand before
you this morning. You see, in God's eyes I'm only a zero with the
rim knocked off." God used this humble servant to impact many
lives, including mine.

I have often wondered, too, if Mr. Hill really believed that his
patience with us unruly kids would one day pay off? To irritate him
in the services, I used to sing as loudly as I could, "Bringing in the
cheese" instead of "Bringing in the sheaves."

During the years as I have shared my testimony, I always point
out that even though I serve as a foreign missionary, I am really a
"home missionary" at heart. Had it not been for faithful home missionaries penetrating the isolated and sparsely populated areas of
northern Michigan with the gospel of Christ, I might not have
been saved. For sure, I would not have served the Lord for 35 years
in Bangladesh. Perhaps that next home you visit will produce a
future pastor or missionary. Faithfulness to our Lord always pays off.

CHAPTER 3

ACCEPTING GOD'S CHALLENGE

*"By faith Abraham, when he was called to go
out into a place which he should after receive
for an inheritance, obeyed: and he went out,
not knowing whither he went."*
Hebrews 11:8

As a young man leaving home, I faced the big challenge of find-ing work, earning an honorable living, and becoming an indepen-dent and resourceful Christian. Little did I realize then that one day I would leave America and spend the hardy years of my life as a missionary in an underdeveloped country called Bangladesh. Many people have asked, "How did you determine God's will for your life?" My reply is always the same and includes these points: willingness, challenges, and circumstances.

After trusting Jesus as my Savior and Lord, I also surrendered myself to be *willing* to serve Him anywhere in the world. There must be a genuine *willingness* to submit to His leading whether it is to stay at home or live abroad.

Before graduating from high school, I had been active in the young people's group of the Lakefield Baptist Church, the one that had its beginning in the cottage on Big Manistique Lake. One Sunday evening in 1948, the pastor scheduled the church's first-ever missionary speaker. Dr. James Norton, missionary appointee to Japan, showed slides of his work, then preached a stirring message from the Word of God. Concluding the service, he challenged us young people, "You who are *willing* to serve the Lord in a foreign land if He should call you, please come and stand with me."

That evening five young people responded, including my future wife and me. At that point in our young lives, we had no idea that one day we would marry and serve a lifetime together in Bangladesh. That *willingness* to be at His disposal at all times is of utmost importance for a fulfilling and fruitful Christian life.

Secondly, for me to say that God *called* me to be a missionary seemed rather nebulous and confusing. There was no audible voice from heaven, no vision. Therefore, I prefer to say that God uses His Word, the Bible, and ordinary men and women of God to *challenge* us. We, then, are to prayerfully consider and accept or reject those challenges.

I have always been impressed with the *challenge* that the God of glory gave to Abram when he was still in Ur of Chaldees (present-day Iraq). God said to him, *"Get thee out of thy country, and from thy kindred, and come into the land which I shall shew thee"* (Acts 7:1).

Abram accepted God's *challenge* which also constituted his *call*. In the same way, I accepted the *challenges* from special men of God to leave my country and my relatives to work in faraway Bangladesh.

Lastly, I share that knowing God's will involves being sensitive and perceptive to the *circumstances* that enter our lives. I have no doubt that the *circumstances* God brought into my life were used by Him to give me direction for future service. I sensed His gracious hand upon me at crucial decision-making times, one of which came shortly after graduating from high school.

I had left the Upper Peninsula of Michigan with a high school friend to seek my fortune working on a farm near Adrian,

Michigan. While I was there the Holy Spirit clearly spoke to me about a new direction for my life. One day as I rode on a tractor-drawn wagon loading bales of hay, I began humming my favorite hymn, "The Way of the Cross Leads Home." Tears flooded my eyes as I thought about my responsibility to a world that needed the Savior. During those sacred moments I decided to leave the farm and pursue a Bible school education; I would enter the ministry.

Returning to the Upper Peninsula, I shared that experience with my pastor, Rev. Marshall Reed, who encouraged me to apply for admission to the Baptist Bible Institute in Grand Rapids, Michigan. Several weeks later I received a letter containing good news and bad news. The good news was that they accepted me for the fall classes of 1950. The bad news was that neither I nor my family had the financial resources to fund my education, or to pay for room and board. Though the odds seemed against me I was willing to take this huge step of faith, confident that He who had called me would provide my needs.

He did just that! In Grand Rapids I contacted Claude and Minnie Jackson, friends of my pastor who had indicated their willingness to help needy Bible school students. They graciously invited me to live with them on their small farm near Ada, Michigan.

The Jacksons had become Christians later in life, after their own children had married and left home. At that stage in their walk with God, they agreed to help this fledgling Bible school student, and I paid for room and board by helping with the evening chores. I had just crossed a huge hurdle!

Each morning on his twenty-mile trip to work in Grand Rapids, Mr. Jackson dropped me off at school. I still have vivid memories of him hunched over the steering wheel of his 1943 green Ford coupe, gas pedal pressed firmly to the floor, racing to get me there by eight o'clock.

To accomplish breakfast, family devotions, and reaching school on time, we had to rise promptly at 6:00 a.m., much too early for me, I thought. More often than not, this undisciplined student fell asleep during the Jacksons' devotional time, which always included a Bible reading, followed by a Bible commentary on the selected passage, then lengthy prayers. Mr. Jackson's monotone followed by Mrs. Jackson's high-pitched voice so early in the morning, produced the same effect on me as today's Sominex™. But those were the "effectual fervent prayers" of two of God's special saints. I have no doubt that they continued to pray for me until the Lord called them to glory, and that whatever success we have since enjoyed is, in part, the fruit of their intercession.

Reflecting on those years, I have often thanked God for that special couple whose generosity and love gave me the incentive, at a critical point in my life, to continue my education and preparation for the ministry. Beginning with that first year on the farm, God proved Himself faithful by allowing me to complete two years of pre-seminary training and three years of seminary in an institution where I was challenged by many missionary speakers. And that wasn't all.

The greatest experience in my life, next to salvation, was meeting Eleanor. My pastor's daughter, she was one of eight children. We first met after her father became the missionary pastor of the Lakefield Baptist Church. I was a junior in high school then and she a sophomore. Though I had my eye on her during our high school days, we parted ways. In the fall of 1950 I went to Grand Rapids to prepare for the ministry. In 1951 she enrolled in the West Suburban Hospital School of Nursing in Oak Park, Illinois.

The saying "opposites attract" certainly proved true in our case. Eleanor is quiet, timid, reserved, and steady. Like Peter, I am more outgoing, even impetuous at times. But as our education proceeded, I knew I was in love with her and, in the end, won her. We were married on July 17, 1954, and began our life together. Before Eleanor's family moved to the Upper Peninsula of Michigan from Ohio, her friends had teased her saying that she would, no doubt, marry an Indian up there. Instead, she got me!

After our marriage, we continued to be interested in foreign missions but, at that juncture, had no special direction. We worked in a church planting project in the town of Lakeview, Michigan, an undertaking that stretched our faith and matured us for the future. Located 54 miles northeast of Grand Rapids, Lakeview had been selected by a group of pastors for a home missions project. With their approval and blessing we began our ministry two weeks before Christmas in 1954. In retrospect, we realized our timing was off. People were more interested in holiday activities than in coming to hear the new preacher in town.

Determined to fight the odds, we began by renting the one-room Village Council Chamber, located in the back of the fire station. To get there, we had to walk between the fire engines. Each Sunday morning before the service, we emptied ashtrays, swept the floor, and aired out the premises.

Our advertisement in the local newspaper brought some results. A family of three joined us for that first Sunday service in the tiny room that reeked of cigar smoke. Even though nobody showed up on the second Sunday, we struggled on through the winter months, gathering a handful of believers. Finding it extremely difficult to develop the work while living miles away in Grand Rapids, we moved to Lakeview in May of 1955. One month later, on Father's Day, Eleanor delivered our first child, a son we named Douglas Jay.

Starting a new church proved to be good training for us, but it was hard going. Attendance was up, then down. When the church eventually began to grow, we found ourselves ministering to a number of lukewarm Christians who refused to be motivated to serve the Lord with any degree of dedication. I don't think we got discouraged more than once a day.

The work grew more rapidly after we left the single room and moved into the Seventh Day Adventist Church. Surprisingly, after some negotiation, the chief elder of that church agreed to lease us their building for $35 a week. After eighteen months of concentrated effort the congregation grew from three people to around fifty-five. A major contributing factor to this growth was my seminary classmate, Reid Minich, who developed a special ministry with the children and young people. Eleanor and I never dreamed then that one day Reid would serve with us in Bangladesh.

Before leaving Lakeview for further education at Wheaton College in Wheaton, Illinois, we officially organized the church, obtained a key piece of property, and built the first phase of a sanctuary. That church later ordained me for the gospel ministry on April 11, 1958.

One day, while living in Lakeview, Eleanor's parents sent a letter inviting us to attend a round-robin missionary conference in Kingsley, Michigan, where they were pastoring. That struck us as a great idea because of our interest in missions, so we loaded our 1948 Mercury sedan and headed north. That evening we listened to the Rev. C. Victor Barnard share his burden for the people of East Pakistan. His message so captivated us that, instead of staying in Kingsley to hear a different missionary, we followed him to the next church. There I mustered up courage to ask him if he would speak in our church at Lakeview, emphasizing that we were a small group and he would be our very first foreign missionary speaker. To my surprise and obvious delight, he agreed.

That Lord's day in September 1955, Victor Barnard spoke to a handful of people. Later, at the dinner table, I thanked him for coming and apologized for the slim attendance. I also assured him that those who were present had appreciated his ministry and challenge. He seized that moment, pointing his finger across the table at us and asking, "What about you? Have you seriously considered giving *your* lives to serve on the far frontiers where few have ever gone? There are millions in East Pakistan who need to hear about Jesus. Today, as I drove through your town, I saw four different churches located within blocks of each other. You won't find that in East Pakistan. God is looking for young people like

you to go where the gospel message has never been preached."
Bam!

We glanced at our first-born son, asleep in a crib at the end of
the table, then promised Rev. Barnard that we would seek God's
will concerning East Pakistan. After our guest had departed, we
knelt together and did just that.

Rev. Barnard, an Australian national, later wrote from East
Pakistan: "I ever maintain that missionary service is priority No.
1. After one has surrendered his life to Christ for service, the first
thought should be, 'Does God want me to be an ambassador on
distant shores?' It's a great honor to stand out here on the frontier
alone with Christ. I think ofttimes that our planning for Christ in
the homeland is wrong when we see churches every five or seven
miles along the highway in the rural areas and hundreds of
churches in the cities with so few to witness for Christ here."

In late summer of 1956 we resigned from the Lakeview church
and moved to Wheaton, where I continued my education for two
more years and where our second child, Linda Marie, was born.
During our time in Wheaton we teamed up with two other college
students, Jerry Leonard and Donald Tyler, to start the Bible
Baptist Church of Naperville, Illinois. This effort continued to
provide Eleanor and me with valuable experience in evangelism
and church planting in the United States. But increasingly we felt
that God was preparing us for a special ministry overseas.

Two weeks before graduation in June of 1958, I found an airmail
letter in my college mailbox. That came as a surprise because normally I found only bills. The letter was postmarked Chittagong,
East Pakistan. I knew immediately it was from Rev. Barnard.
Excited, yet nervous, I read it amidst the jostling of the other students. His opening line jumped out at me: "COME OVER AND
HELP US"—the very words of the apostle Paul's Macedonian
vision.

Rev. Barnard's letter went on to tell of needy tribes living in the
hills along the East Pakistan/Burma border. Tribal groups with

names such as Tipperahs, Marmas, and Murungs were waiting for someone to tell them of Jesus and His love. Missionary recruits were urgently needed to take up the task of evangelizing these people.

He wrote: "A great challenge awaits you. Here is this great city (Chittagong) of 300,000 and only a feeble witness for Christ. Then lie the plains of the interior with four million people in our districts of Chittagong and Noakhali without a single witness of Christ. Off the coast we have a number of islands with a total population of perhaps 400,000 without a missionary and perhaps no witness for Christ has ever visited these islands. Last week Mrs. Barnard and I stopped off at two islands and so queer were our faces to these people that we couldn't get a minute's peace. Even whilst we were eating they stood around and gazed upon us. We were a spectacle unto men if not unto angels. We again went up the Sangu River to a point about 50 miles from its estuary and stayed at Bandarban. Our hearts burned within us as we heard of the untouched tribes ten days' journey up the river and away on the rugged mountains that form the uncharted borders of Burma and East Pakistan."

He went on to remind us, "It seemed to me that God spoke to you some two years back when I was with you. If God has called, He will deepen that sense of call as you definitely seek the Divine will. Two things I say—don't come here if God has not called, for you will never stick to it. Secondly, don't stay at home if God has called, for He looks to you to answer at the judgment if you say 'no' to the heavenly vision. If you feel that the Lord is turning your footsteps this way, then you should be making plans to come over."

I folded that letter and tucked it into my pocket. After completing a class in missions led by Dr. E. Meyers Harrison, formerly a missionary to Burma, I hurried home to Eleanor. Before revealing the letter, I asked her again what she thought we should be doing with our lives.

"I think we ought to be involved in foreign missions," she replied.

"Any special field in mind?" I probed.

Her reply sent shivers down my spine as she said, "Since Rev. Barnard spoke in our church in Lakeview, I haven't been able to get East Pakistan off my mind."

With those words I sensed God confirming His call to us. I then handed her Rev. Barnard's letter. After reading it, she agreed that we should initiate a plan of action that would take us to East Pakistan. That evening we sat together and composed a letter to his mission, the Association of Baptists for World Evangelism, Inc. (ABWE), requesting application papers. It was clear that God was using these new special *circumstances* to direct us to the field of His choosing.

The minutes of ABWE's semi-annual board meeting of October 14-16, 1958 read, "Mr. and Mrs. Walsh gave individual testimonies as to Christian experience, subsequent training and missionary call. After the usual period of questioning, Dr. Joseph Stowell led in prayer, and the Walshes were excused. After some discussion, it was moved, seconded and voted #2545 that Mr. and Mrs. David J. Walsh be accepted as missionaries of the ABWE. It was moved, seconded, and voted #2546 that Mr. and Mrs. Walsh be appointed to the East Pakistan field."

Before us now lay the formidable task of raising our support, which we began to do shortly after the birth of our third child, Debra Joy, who brought a special joy to our lives on a blustery November day. At that critical point in my life I had a wife and three small children, no job or income, and Christmas was just ahead. Yet Eleanor and I possessed a strong desire to move forward, trusting God to provide our needs. During 1959 we presented our missionary vision in more than 100 churches from Hackensack, New Jersey to Newberry, Michigan to St. Louis, Missouri. After eleven months of deputation, we were cleared to leave. Against all odds we embarked for Hebron on January 29, 1960.

In January 1959, Rev. Barnard penned a letter from Hebron, our future home, which helped us greatly. He wrote, "This, our first letter of the new year, brings with it greetings from Hebron, our new mission station in the jungle. We arrived here at night on Christmas Eve after a journey by sea and river lasting exactly four days.

"On arrival here we had the job of clearing and cleaning the jungle land and each day, except the Lord's Day, sees some progress in erecting our houses and other mission buildings. These are of simple design and construction—lumber from the forest and bamboo from the jungles. As we have at present only a very small plot of land on the river bank, we are asking the Lord to give us a larger area whereupon we can establish the Mission. We have made application for some government owned land. Pray that we may receive favor from the officials and that the land will be granted to us."

CHAPTER 4

A GRAVEYARD PRAYER

"So Abram departed, as the Lord had spoken
unto him . . . And Abram took Sarai his
wife . . . and they went forth to go into the
land of Canaan; and into the land of Canaan
they came."
Genesis 12:4,5

The *Hellenic Splendor* dropped anchor in Chittagong's outer harbor on the night of March 16, 1960. We could hardly contain our excitement as we stood on deck viewing the lights of Chittagong city in the distance. At flood tide the following morning, a Bengali pilot boarded the ship and slowly guided the ship up the Karnaphuli River to jetty No. 17 where we moored. Standing on the dock under a blazing sun, and waving white handkerchiefs of welcome, were Rev. and Mrs. Barnard and daughter, and Mrs. Helen Miller and her four children. They were East Pakistan's faithful pioneers and our co-workers.

After filling out numerous forms for Customs and Immigration officials, we were allowed to disembark and join our waiting colleagues. As we embraced each one we were keenly aware that they had recently buried loved ones in Chittagong's international cemetery. On January 24, 1958, the Barnards' lovely 14-year-old daughter, Winifred Mary, died of peritonitis following an appendectomy.

On May 3, 1959, only 10 months before our arrival, Helen Miller's husband, Paul, died suddenly of bulbar polio. He had said good-bye to Helen and the children, leaving Hebron by boat to care for business in Chittagong where he became ill. His family never saw him again because in a hot, tropical climate, burial within twenty-four hours after death is imperative.

In a tribute to Paul Miller, his friend and fellow missionary Rev. Barnard wrote: "Just the other day Paul waved a cheery good-bye to all of us here on the Hebron compound and made his way across the rice fields to Lama, enroute to Chittagong to attend to some mission business. A canoe awaited him there to take him down river on the first stage of his journey. As the hollowed-out tree trunk drifted downstream, Paul lifted his heart to God in prayer thinking of his wife and little ones, the work of God he loved so much, the coming glory of Christ, and then quietly committed himself to the Father's safe keeping. Just after midnight the canoe reached Cheringa. Paul waited for the morning light to board an ancient WW II vehicle which does service in these parts as a bus. After a horrible jolting journey over a rough road he arrived at Dohazari, the railhead. Crossing the river he boarded the train on the last stage of his journey. After another three hours he reached Chittagong, worn, tired, and sick.

"His fellow missionaries there did their utmost to quiet the fever and give him rest. On the fourth day it was decided to send him to Dhaka where better treatment could be obtained. The tired and sick missionary was placed on board the train in company with another missionary and jolted along the tracks for another 200 miles.

"At the Holy Family Hospital his condition was diagnosed and the verdict given: polio. Everything possible was done, even to the flying in of an iron lung from Karachi, 1100 miles away, an act of kindness on the part of the American Consul and military authorities there. However, at about 7:30 p.m. on the Lord's Day evening, May 3, the royal summons came and Paul Miller 'was not' for God took him. His 'earthly tabernacle' was brought down to Chittagong and laid near to that of our own precious daughter, Mary, and there they lie until the trumpet call."

Eleanor and I had eagerly looked forward to working with the Barnards and Millers in tribal evangelism. As it turned out, that would not happen. Within two months of our arrival, both families left East Pakistan for medical and personal reasons. They never returned to work there, although they continued to serve the Lord in other areas of the world.

The day after our arrival in Chittagong, missionary colleagues drove us to the international cemetery to view the graves of their loved ones. As we approached the freshly placed markers, a holy hush fell on us. A few silent, tear-filled moments passed as we joined hands in a circle around the graves. Then Victor Barnard's steady, courageous voice broke the silence, "Let's pray together."

Our heads dropped instantly as he began a prayer we shall never forget: "Gracious, loving, and merciful heavenly Father", he prayed, "We stand here today around the graves of these your precious children. Our hearts ache, O Lord, because they are gone from us; but we rejoice in knowing that they are in Your presence. You alone, O Lord, know of the silent tears that have stained our pillows and the emptiness that has filled our hearts. Oh, how we miss them. But, gracious Father, again today we commit it all to You. You said in Your holy Word that unless a corn of wheat fall to the earth and die, it abides alone and will not bring forth fruit. O Lord, bring forth from the lives of these Thy precious children, much fruit in this needy land. Keep us faithful until that day when we shall meet You face to face. Amen."

What a sobering experience to begin our missionary career. It helped, however, to put things into perspective as we faced the future. There would be recurring health problems with which to contend. To avoid contracting hepatitis, typhoid, and diarrheal diseases, we would learn to boil our drinking water for the rest of our years in Bangladesh. Because mosquito-borne malaria is a lurking menace, we would have to swallow bitter quinine pills every week for all our years there. We would also have to contend with some of the same perils that the apostle Paul mentioned in 2 Corinthians 11:26 ". . . in perils of waters, in perils of robbers, in perils by the heathen, in perils in the city, in perils in the wilderness, and in perils in the sea." We would have many adjustments to make as we established ourselves in our adopted land.

Our first taste of culture shock came as we rode with the reception party from the port area to mission headquarters in central Chittagong. It was dusk as we rode into town. Flickering kerosene lanterns lit the tiny shops. The streets teemed with people, mostly men (Bangladesh is a Muslim land where *purdah,* the religious and social practice of secluding women, is observed.) That year of our arrival, March was Islam's most holy month of *Ramazan* when faithful Muslims abstain from eating, drinking, and smoking from dawn to dusk. At first we found it repulsive to see and hear people hacking and spitting all day long. We later learned that their religion prohibited them from swallowing even their own saliva lest *Allah* (God) nullify the merits of their fast.

Throughout the entire month at sunset, fasting crowds poured into the narrow streets of the city to break fast with *Iftar* (breakfast). *Iftar* includes lighting cigarettes, eating finger foods, and drinking tea. Then, from sunset until dawn, we listened to the revelry as families gorged themselves with rice and spicy curries. As we analyzed it, *Ramazan* simply switched the normal daytime eating schedule to the nighttime hours. Rather suddenly we realized that we were foreigners in a strange land with religions, customs, and culture vastly different from ours. Like it or not, we were the ones who would have to adapt.

Over the years many people in North America asked about the difficulty our children had in adjusting to the customs and culture of Bangladesh. Our answer has always been, "Practically none. It was we adults who had the problems!"

Early on we had to acclimate ourselves to sleeping under mosquito nets. At first they seemed cumbersome and confining and, above all, a nuisance to manipulate. The pesky mosquitoes seemingly possessed built-in radar that could locate any port of entry in the netting. Eventually we found that nets not only gave us protection from prowling insects but also provided a sense of security.

Our first night in Chittagong was a nightmare. Advised in advance by fellow missionaries, we had packed mosquito nets in our luggage to be readily available for use. That night we put the children to bed and securely fastened their nets, confident that they would be safe from mosquitoes and bugs. In the morning, however, to our consternation, we found their arms and legs peppered with bites as if they had contracted chicken pox. The mosquitoes bit them when they rolled up against the nets.

Mosquito nets not only shielded us from mosquitoes, of which there were legion, but also cockroaches that crawled out in droves after dark. That first night in Chittagong I nearly broke my neck after slipping on one while walking to the bathroom with a candle. We soon understood why the Bengali people called them *tela pokas* (oily bugs). We never really learned how to conquer the cockroach problem. It was always disconcerting to wake up in the morning and see one of those persistent creatures straddling my toothbrush!

Mosquito nets protected us from yet another problem—geckos. The Bengalis call them *tick-tickies* because of the "tick-tick" sounds they make when communicating with each other. Each evening these little lizards crawl out of their hiding places to feast on mosquitoes and cockroaches. Because of this, they became our special friends. However, from time to time in their determined efforts to snap up their prey, they would lose their suction-cup grip and fall on our nets.

During our first eight years in Bangladesh the security factor of mosquito nets could not be overestimated. In later years, as screening and bug sprays became available, our dependence on mosquito nets vanished, although at times we wished we still had them.

Volumes have been written on culture shock and the many ways in which life in a land such as Bangladesh is totally different from life in the West. Many missionaries, unable to cope with such adjustments, have returned to their homelands defeated. Rudyard Kipling's famous line, "East is East and West is West, and ne'er the twain shall meet" was composed with great insight into the customs and cultures of the Indian subcontinent. Though twentieth century western culture has penetrated India and Bangladesh to some degree, there remains a basic resistance to modern ways. This is especially true as it relates to customs deeply rooted in the religions of Islam, Hinduism, and Buddhism.

A person's success in any foreign missionary endeavor and his ability to enjoy longevity of service, as well as find joy and contentment in the work, depends greatly on his or her success in adapting to different living conditions, learning the language fluently, and participating in the culture of the land, as long as these are not unethical, unhealthy, or unbiblical.

CHAPTER 5

SATAN'S DARTS

*"But they that wait upon the Lord shall renew
their strength; they shall mount up with wings
like eagles; they shall run, and not be weary;
and they shall walk, and not faint."*
Isaiah 40:31

Before embarking on our missionary career, Eleanor and I had been cautioned by godly men and women that Satan would test us. We were admonished to prepare for the spiritual warfare so vividly described in Ephesians chapter six. We were grateful for this caution, but little did we realize the subtle ways in which we would be tested.

By the time we arrived in Chittagong in 1960, Eleanor was seven months pregnant with our fourth child. Our missionary colleagues in Chittagong had decided that, due to the lack of good hospital facilities in East Pakistan, we should travel to Lahore, West Pakistan, for the delivery.

After only two weeks in Chittagong, we packed our bags again for the 1,200 mile trip across India to West Pakistan, taking with us our newly hired language teacher, Benu Pundit. The language committee was serious about our learning Bengali. Rev. Barnard made arrangements for our family to fly from Chittagong to Lahore via Dhaka. He and Benu journeyed by train to Dhaka to make overnight guest house reservations before meeting us at the airport. The Lahore flight was scheduled for the following day.

On our arrival in Dhaka at sundown, Rev. Barnard was waiting with a taxi to escort us to a guest house located in the older section of the city. Our family of five squeezed like sardines into the back seat of that ancient vehicle along with our luggage. Rev. Barnard sat in front with the driver and the driver's assistant, whose main duty was to push the car to get it started.

The driver, obviously pleased with his load of foreigners, and endeavoring to impress us, accelerated his speed as we wove our way through Dhaka's crowded streets. Suddenly, a man carrying a huge brass pot on his head stepped in front of the taxi. I yelled to alert the driver but he obviously didn't understand an American yell or else failed to see the danger. We hit that poor fellow with a sickening thud, sending him sprawling to the street along with his load of milk. Almost instantly an excited and noisy crowd surrounded our taxi, shining lights and peering at us through the windows. We sat there like animals in a cage, petrified, until a policeman arrived. After warning us not to say a single word about the accident lest we get tied up in a court case, Rev. Barnard got out of the taxi and spoke to the policeman in Bengali. After a few anxious moments he and the policeman squeezed into the front seat with the driver and we proceeded to our destination. The driver's assistant was left standing in the crowd.

At the guest house Rev. Barnard had a few more private words with the policeman and driver before they drove off into the night. We heard nothing more of the injured milkman and could only guess that the policeman had been gratified with a substantial *baksheesh* (bribe) provided by the driver.

Arriving in Lahore we were received at the airport by fellow ABWE missionaries Juanita Canfield and Miriam Morin, on temporary assignment studying the Islamic religion. They had graciously arranged interim lodging in their home until we could find our own accommodations. After hunting several days, we located an apartment near the United Christian Hospital where our baby would be born.

May 16, 1960 dawned blazing hot. At 8:00 a.m. the thermometer had already registered 105° and by noon it was 117°. At lunch that day Eleanor began feeling light contractions which neither of us took too seriously. But within minutes after putting the children down for a nap, she put me on evacuation alert. Her contractions were getting more regular so I jumped on a bicycle to notify Juanita and Miriam, who had agreed to care for the children while Eleanor was in the hospital. Unable to find a taxi, I hailed a three-wheeled motorized tricycle. Eleanor later wrote her parents about this experience, "Jay couldn't get a taxi so we came to the hospital by a motorcycle carriage. It was a bit bumpy but faster than a *tonga* (horse drawn cart) and less smelly."

We arrived at the hospital at 3:00 p.m. and an hour later I was summoned from the waiting room by a Pakistani nurse. Eleanor had given birth to a baby boy. Phillip Martin, our second son, was delivered by Dr. Martin, a Scottish lady. Although we actually named Phillip Martin after my brother, Martin, we are certain the doctor thought we named our son after her.

Before leaving the hospital, Dr. Martin gave us two pieces of unsolicited advice. The first was that we should have no more children. "Your supporters won't stand for it," she scolded.

And, because of the heat wave that was gripping Lahore, she advised, "You should leave here as soon as possible and move to a higher, cooler elevation in the mountains. The weather here is much too hot for the baby."

To say that Lahore was a hot place to live would be a gross understatement. During our weeks there, daily temperatures ranged between 105° and 120° Fahrenheit. Before retiring for a night's sleep, we soaked sheets in a tub of water, wrung them out, then stretched them over us for a cooling effect. Under the swirling ceiling fan, they dried within a few minutes. We then repeated the procedure.

Lahore's high temperatures occur because the city lies in the desert at the foot of the mighty Himalaya Mountains. Most of

Pakistan's foreign community, as well as high-placed government workers, leave the desert plains during the hottest months and move to cooler hill stations in the mountains. Murree, Pakistan, located 7,000 feet above sea level, where our children would one day attend high school, was a favorite spot.

Doctor Martin had given us good advice, but we were puzzled as to how to implement it. Then, in God's perfect timing, Eleanor received a letter from missionary nurse Jean Sodemann who served with The Evangelical Alliance Mission's (TEAM) hospital near Abbottabad. After learning that Eleanor and I were in Lahore, Jean invited us to join her in Mansehra, a small town located at an elevation of 4,000 feet in Pakistan's northwest frontier province. Jean and Eleanor had been classmates at the West Suburban Hospital School of Nursing in Oak Park, Illinois, and had graduated together in 1954.

"It's much cooler up here," Jean wrote. "I sure hope you can come."

Her invitation arrived when we needed it most, and we felt confident that it was from the Lord. After officially registering Phillip's birth with the American Consulate in Lahore, necessary to make him an American citizen, we traveled by train to what was then Pakistan's capital city, Rawalpindi, and from there by bus to Mansehra. The train journey was difficult, but the bus trip was a nightmare. Unfortunately, we lost our language teacher, Benu, who had disembarked during the night at the wrong station and didn't catch up to us for two more days. We had been depending on him to help us with the language barrier.

After boarding a battered old bus crowded with people heading for the hospital and points north, we left Rawalpindi and were soon in the mountains. I clearly remember looking out one side of the bus where it was possible to reach through the window and touch the mountain, and out the other side to see a valley thousands of feet below. Perhaps we were too numb to be frightened. To make our journey even more tense, there were several inches of play in the steering wheel. That nuisance kept the driver busy on a winding road, barely wide enough for two vehicles to pass.

The hill station of Mansehra didn't quite meet our expectations either, although it was certainly much cooler. When the bus chugged to a halt at the station, a group of turbaned coolies descended on our luggage tearing at it like jackals on a carcass. We watched in horror thinking that everything would be ripped to shreds. Much to our relief, the skillful driver intervened and selected two men from the group. He also explained the reason for their aggressiveness: a foreigner's *baksheesh* (tip) was usually much more substantial than their own countrymen would give.

"They all wanted to carry your luggage," he explained. "You Americans have plenty of money." If he only knew!

After seeking directions, we proceeded up the hill, through the bazaar, to the TEAM mission compound. Jean was there and welcomed us like long-lost friends. We were overjoyed to see another American. We spent several hours sharing news over a cup of tea before she showed us to our rooms.

Our living accommodations were in a small compound near the upper end of the bazaar. Jean's mission had used it at one time for a Christian bookroom and counseling center. Now empty, it contained a half dozen small rooms, each facing onto an enclosed courtyard that was open to the sky.

Our congenial hostess first showed us the kitchen which contained a greasy black two-burner kerosene stove perched on an equally greasy black table. There was no other furniture in that room. The next cubicle contained an empty barrel which, she explained, a coolie would fill with water every day. She then displayed a coin to show us how much we should pay him for each trip.

Two of the other rooms were bedrooms containing Pakistani beds, fabricated of ropes which drooped to the floor, much like a hammock. Lastly, Jean showed us the toilet—a clay pot in the corner of the last cubical. "Don't worry," she explained, "a sweeper will come each morning to empty it."

No sooner had Jean completed our orientation then the gate to the bazaar swung open. A turbaned, wall-eyed coolie came puffing in with a goat's skin full of water strapped to his back. He walked over to the empty barrel, released his hold on the goat's neck, and water gurgled out. Jean made sure we paid him, then left us to unpack our bags with a cheery, "Have a good night! See you in the morning."

Our terrible experience in Dhaka, the nerve-racking bus trip to Mansehra, the luggage episode in the bazaar, and now seeing our "motel" accommodations was too much for me. I was sure Eleanor must be as depressed as I. After Jean was safely out of hearing distance I vented my feelings. "Honey," I said, "let's go back home!" And I meant America. In her calm way she replied, "Why don't we wait until morning?"

That was a sleepless night as I mulled over recent events, wondering if we had made a mistake in leaving our homeland. I rose at dawn, dressed, and walked up the mountain road leading out of the bazaar. The coolness of the morning impressed me favorably after the stifling heat we had left behind in Lahore. A thin fog hung in the air as I strolled along, face to the ground, praying and thinking. After a short distance I paused and lifted my eyes. There, to my awe and amazement, looming up before me were the mighty, snow-capped, Himalaya Mountains! K2, the world's second-highest mountain, stood like a giant in the background. At that moment the Holy Spirit melted my heart. Tears gushed from my eyes and streamed down my face. Spontaneously I began singing:

> O Lord my God, when I in awesome wonder,
> Consider all the worlds Thy hands have made,
> I see the stars, I hear the rolling thunder,
> Thy power throughout the universe displayed:
> Then sings my soul, my Savior God, to Thee:

How great Thou art, How great Thou art!
Then sings my soul, my Savior God, to Thee:
How great Thou art, How great Thou art!

In that special moment it was as if the Lord Himself said to me, "Jay, why are you so concerned about a greasy black kerosene stove, drooping rope beds, drinking water carried in goat skins, and a crude pottery toilet? Am I not the God of the Himalayas? Have I not created those lofty mountains you are seeing for the very first time? Don't give up. Take courage. I am your God, and I have work for you to do."

Revived in spirit, I returned to my family a different man. My attitude had changed, and I was ready to face the future regardless of the hardships it might entail—as, indeed, there were many to come.

Thinking back, my childhood prepared me for some of those hardships. Born and raised in a poor family in Michigan's sparsely populated Upper Peninsula, I had learned early how to cope with poverty. We struggled to keep food on the table and clothes on our backs. We hunted, fished, and trapped to make ends meet. My father, Phineas Jay, was known to his many friends as Huckleberry Phin. While working in Flint, Michigan, in the Fisher Body car plant, he broke his back. That accident forever disabled him from doing strenuous work although he picked up various jobs when he was able. Eventually he found employment as a fire tower guard with the Michigan Department of Natural Resources. Even so, money was hard to come by and, like many poor people in the U.P., we struggled to make a living.

Until I graduated from high school, my family lived in a one-room log cabin with 224 square feet of living space. Though the six of us were cramped, we were basically happy and contented. I could never agree with those who propagate the theory that disease, crime, and unhappiness is synonymous with being poor. That might be the case for some, but millions of poor people understand that having wealth doesn't necessarily bring happiness. While living in the log cabin, my family found Christ and that made all the difference in our lives. True peace and contentment come from knowing Him, not from having wealth and possessions. I firmly believe that my background, and whatever hardships we suffered as a family during my youth, prepared me for a life of service in the extremely poor country of Bangladesh.

In those early days our call was severely tested as Eleanor and I adapted to a totally different way of life. But through it all, God graciously showed us that He was greater than circumstances, and that we could trust Him for the future.

Shortly into our stay at Mansehra, colleague Gene Gurganus cabled me to return to East Pakistan as soon as possible. Gene and his wife Elizabeth (who was always called Beth by fellow missionaries) arrived in Bangladesh in 1958 and had made plans to live at Hebron. He needed help to complete a building project—a house that we Walshes would eventually occupy in Hebron—so he could pack up and reunite with his family in the USA. Beth and their two little daughters had returned to America several weeks earlier because of a medical emergency. Sensing the urgency of his cable, I left Eleanor and the children in Mansehra, flew back across India, and joined Gene in Hebron. I am not sure that Eleanor has ever forgiven me for being so dedicated!

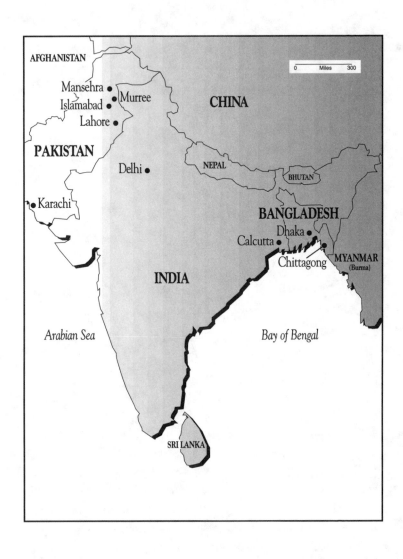

CHAPTER 6

FINDING OUR OWN "HEBRON"

"Then Abram removed his tent, and came and
dwelt by the oaks of Mamre, which is in
Hebron, and built there an altar to the Lord."
Genesis 13:18

If ABWE was to successfully evangelize the numerous tribes living in the rugged hills along Bangladesh's borders with Burma and India, we would need a convenient center from which to operate. Hebron became that place.

Prior to 1947 when Great Britain carved the state of Pakistan out of India as a homeland for the Muslims, the British Raj had allocated an area solely for minority tribal peoples, similar to an Indian reservation in North America. Lying on the western flank of the Arakan Yomas mountain system, the area is composed of rugged terrain with long, picturesque valleys and hills which have stood for centuries as silent sentinels over the undisturbed sanctuaries of various tribes: Chakma, Marma, Tipperah, Murung, Kumi, Chak, Khyang, and Bawm. This scenic land in southeastern Bangladesh is known as the Chittagong Hill Tracts. Comprising approximately 5,138 square miles, it constitutes nearly one-tenth of Bangladesh's total land area.

The Hill Tracts District stretches from the town of Ramgarh in the north to Teknaf in the south. The northern Hill Tracts border the Indian states of Tripura and Mizoram. The southern section borders the district of Arakan, Burma (now known as Myanmar). The entire area is a mass of sub-tropical jungle, fed by heavy monsoon rains, where a wild profusion of birds and beasts breed in the narrow valleys flanked by steep hills and criss-crossed with rivers and streams.

On a 1957 survey trip to the southern end of the Chittagong Hill Tracts District, Rev. and Mrs. Barnard and Rev. Paul Miller, exhausted from their thirteen-day trek through rugged tribal country, arrived at a government outpost called Lama, located on the banks of the Matamahari River. Lama, which might be compared to a county seat town, had a police station, a post office, and a bi-weekly bazaar. The tired missionaries were graciously received by government officials, served hot tea, and provided with overnight accommodations. The following morning was market day in Lama. Merchants from up and down the river arrived by country boat with merchandise to barter, trade or sell to the tribal people who trekked in from the surrounding hills. Marmas, Tipperahs, and Murungs, distinctively dressed in their native garb, carried their products to sell: rice, cotton, tobacco, brooms, wild honey, *choan* (elephant grass), and chickens.

Observing that mixture of colorful tribes gathering in one place, the missionaries were quick to recognize Lama as a key spot for tribal evangelism. Since purchasing property in the Chittagong Hill Tracts District was prohibited by law, the missionaries decided to select a site as near as possible to Lama in the adjoining Chittagong District.

Studying a crude map of the area, they were delighted to discover that only a mile from Lama, along the same Matamahari River, a promontory of land lay within Chittagong District where there were no restrictions on land purchase. That huge land mass, composed of two main areas called Bilchari and Boro Bomu, is surrounded by the Chittagong Hill Tracts, yet connected to the Chittagong District by the Matamahari River. Satisfied that this was an ideal location for a mission station, the weary missionary party returned 75 miles to their home base in Chittagong to share the news with their colleagues.

Several months later, in 1958, after Rev. Barnard located an elderly Muslim gentleman willing to sell his land, approval was granted by the ABWE to proceed with purchasing a jungle-covered plot on the banks of the Matamahari River near a Buddhist village called Bilchari.

The field council minutes of October 24, 1958 state: "Discussion was held on the offer of property on the Matamahari River above Lama, situated in an enclave of the Chittagong District, but surrounded by the Hill Tracts District. The site is considered excellent as a base for work among the hill tribes. It was voted that Rev. Barnard acquire the property of approximately two-thirds of an acre at the price of Rupees 600.00, the purchase to be concluded at an early date in Rev. Barnard's name, but to be acquired by the ABWE as soon as practicable (Rupees 600.00 is $127.00)."

The official minutes of December 10, 1958 state, "The land was acquired and the title transferred on November 7, 1958."

The hand of God was clearly upon this purchase. It has meant that, throughout subsequent years, while travel in the Chittagong Hill Tracts has been restricted, ABWE has been able to use Hebron as a base for reaching the tribes.

On Christmas Eve 1958, a lonely canoe pushed its way up the Matamahari River with a missionary, his wife, and little daughter aboard. It had been a long journey from Chittagong city by *sampan* (a bulky, cargo-carrying boat) down the Karnaphuli River to the Bay of Bengal, then southward along the coast for 60 miles to the Matamahari River, and finally a journey of 25 miles up that river to Bilchari. Tired, dirty and hungry, the travelers arrived at the site after four days and three nights. As night fell, they stepped ashore on a freshly cut piece of jungle land right at the door of tribal country and claimed the land for the Lord Jesus Christ. They named their little plot of ground "Hebron," remembering all

the precious promises of the everlasting God to the ancient patriarch Abraham.

Thirty-three years later, in 1991, Mrs. Barnard wrote about
their experience which led to the opening of a mission station
named Hebron. "We at once began to gather things which we
knew were not possible to obtain in those jungles. The day arrived
when we could leave Chittagong. The boat was packed, leaving
room on the deck where we would spend the night. When we
boarded the boat, which was night time, the *majis* (boatmen) told
us that the river police would possibly ask who was in the boat,
and that we definitely should not answer them as they would possibly rob us.

"Sure enough, when we were in mid-stream, the police called
out, 'Who goes there?' The boatman called back, 'The Inspector
of Police.' And they said, 'Pass on.' Before long we were right out
into the sea. It was kind of frightening in the darkness of night.

"We had traveled all night and most of the next day when we
came to the Matamahari River, which wasn't deep enough for our
boat. So everything had to be unloaded into twelve small canoes.
Our fleet of small boats pushed up the river until evening, and, as
we were in the jungles, where would we sleep?

"We spread out on the river bank those lovely patchwork quilts
which used to be made for missionaries by their sending churches.
The moon was beautifully bright. I asked, 'Who will put out the
light when we're in bed?'

"We were up bright and early next morning because we still had
another ten hours of travel to reach Bilchari. The poor boatmen
were hungry and there were no eating places or even homes along
this journey. We left them to cook their rice and pushed on ahead.

"When we reached the chosen place at 10:00 p.m. that night,
we came to a small group of jungle homes, and at the arrival of
twelve boats an elderly Hindu gentleman, hearing all the commotion, came to the river's edge to see what was happening. He
asked, 'Where will you stay?' (We knew no one). I said, 'Last night

we slept on the river bank.' He said, 'No, you can't do that here; there are too many wild animals.' He told us he had a small room we could use and then the dear man cooked rice for us. He was always a dear friend.

"We tried to sleep. The next morning was Christmas Day. Our new friend called up workers to clear a small patch of jungle ground so the tent could be put up, as we were burning hot under a straw roof. We soon got settled in. Camping wasn't a problem. Our Christmas dinner was a can of baked beans and pork, but we never found the pork. Still it was good.

"They were hard days and, I guess, exciting, such as cooking our curry over an open fire when a big old crow swooped down and took his share out of the pan. But they were wonderful days seeing the faces of the dear men when they first heard about the Lord. My husband would say each time, 'When you go home, tell your wives as much as you can remember and your families also.'"

Speaking of their tribal experiences, Mrs. Barnard concludes, "Yes, they were great days even if we had to walk hundreds of miles. Nothing that is done for the Lord is lost."

That initial penetration into tribal country by the Barnards and Millers, and the purchase of Hebron as a base for evangelism, laid the foundation for years of fruitful ministry among the tribes living in the hill country along the Bangladesh/Burma border.

CHAPTER 7

DRIVING IN OUR STAKES

*"By faith he sojourned in the land of promise,
as in a strange country, dwelling in tabernacles
with Isaac and Jacob, the heirs with him of the
same promise."*

Hebrews 11:9

After Phillip's birth and our sojourn in West Pakistan, the Field Council decided that we should move to Hebron right away for two reasons. First, Eleanor and I were called to the tribal work. That had been Rev. Barnard's original challenge to us when he visited our church in Michigan in 1956. Since Hebron was to become the mission's tribal headquarters, we wanted to be there anyway.

Secondly, fellow missionary Gene Gurganus, whose wife and children had returned to the USA for emergency medical care, was eager to join his family. He needed to turn the fledgling Hebron work over to us as soon as possible. No other missionary man was available to carry on the spiritual ministries, and to complete the building projects that had been started.

Our move to Hebron would also provide security for the two single missionaries already living there. Bangladesh is a male-dominated society where women are under a man's protection. If they have no male protector, they might be harassed or abused. I would, as Gene had done, be fulfilling that protector role for Mary Lou Brownell and Joyce Ann Wingo.

Mary Lou, a registered nurse, had moved to Hebron in the fall of 1959 to continue the medical work that Helen Miller had started before Paul's death. Joyce Ann, a linguist, had moved there because of her burden for the Tipperah people and her desire to translate the Bible for them. She was the first missionary to learn their dialect.

When we arrived on the scene, Joyce Ann had already compiled a simple dictionary and translated the gospel of John in phonetic script. In the weeks and months to follow, Eleanor and I would work closely with those two women.

In August 1960, after Eleanor and the children had returned from Mansehra, we moved to Hebron. We traveled 60 tortuous miles south from Chittagong on the single lane Arakan highway to the town of Cheringa, located near the Matamahari River. There we hired country boats, long cigar-shaped canoes, for the rest of the ten-hour journey. The canoes, deftly propelled along by *majis* (boatmen) using long bamboo poles, were our only means of transportation into the interior.

Strong, sinewy coolies helped me load the boats with 16 barrels of personal and household goods, a gasoline-powered Maytag washer, and a kerosene operated refrigerator: nearly all of our worldly possessions. Those supplies were to last for our first four-year term. Before leaving the USA, Eleanor had the monumental task of estimating the sizes of clothing the children would need during each of those years.

Upon reaching Hebron, the boats moored in front of the bamboo shanty that we would call home. Benu, our language teacher, hired a crew of local villagers to carry our goods up the muddy river bank to the house. They were a scrawny group of men, barefooted and scantily clothed, obviously very poor. We couldn't help but notice their interest and curiosity at the amount of material goods we possessed. Later on, when we visited their humble huts, we could understand how "rich" we must have looked in their eyes. How could we compare our lifestyles? They could carry all their worldly possessions on their backs if the occasion so demanded. We, on the other hand, were encumbered with those 16 barrels of supplies and that shiny new equipment.

The thought of living as "rich" American missionaries among the poor people of the hills caused me to wonder how we could reach them with the gospel. It would be next to impossible for them to rise to our standard of living. Nor could we live as they did and remain healthy. One day, with these thoughts troubling me, I asked our language teacher the burning question on my heart.

"Benu," I said, "I never before realized how rich we are and how poor your people are until we moved here. In America, people with my salary would be considered quite poor. Tell me, how are we going to reach your people for the Lord?"

Benu lowered his head in deep thought. Seconds later, looking me straight in the eye, he replied, "My people will know if you love them."

Wow, I could hardly believe my ears! His thoughtful reply struck home and provided the answer I needed. Even though his people would never live on our standard—nor we on theirs—the great gulf between us could be spanned by Christian love. At that point I determined to learn to speak their language as they spoke it, eat their food as they prepared it, and welcome them into our home as friends and equals. Over the years we have continued that policy and found that it works.

A short time after our arrival in Hebron, Gene Gurganus turned his responsibilities over to me, including the jobs of acting Field Chairman and Treasurer. With the Barnards, Millers and Gurganuses gone, we five-month-old "veterans" found ourselves in charge, not only of Hebron but the whole mission. This meant assuming responsibility for completing several unfinished building projects, and handling mission business while continuing language study.

Before he left for North Carolina, Gene thoughtfully gave me a quick language lesson. Holding up a hammer he said, "This is a *matool.*" After I repeated that word several times for him, he showed me a nail which was a *pereck.* Finally, he hoisted a hand saw which was a *kawrut.* With that he grinned, said good-bye, then boarded a country boat for the 15-mile ride downriver enroute to the USA. Armed with the new vocabulary words, I started my missionary career at Hebron.

Our first task was to get settled into our home. The house on the river bank, though ample in size, was made of woven bamboo with a thatched roof and a mud floor. In that indigenous accommodation, Eleanor faced the challenge of making a home for the family. That wasn't easy. We had no well or running water, nor did we have an inside toilet. Our source of water was the Matamahari River, flowing in a westerly direction past the front door. To solve the water problem, we hired a tribal man named Langrau Murung who carried water from the river to fill several 55-gallon barrels parked in one corner of the house.

Before leaving America, we had obtained two additional tidbits of worthy advice. The first was that we should take along our sense of humor and leave behind our sense of smell. That definitely had merit, but the second piece of advice was far more practical: In order to kill harmful bacteria, we should boil the water for at least 10 minutes before drinking it.

One day Langrau came running to the house and excitedly called me to the river's edge where he pointed to some colored cloth snagged on a branch in the river. He was suspicious and wanted me to investigate. Wading out to take a closer look, I found a human body.

"Hurry," I said to him with a sense of urgency, "Let's report this to the police."

"No use," he answered, "likely it is they who have done it." He then gave the snag a kick and the body floated away. When I reported this to Eleanor, she started boiling our drinking water for 20 minutes! A major adjustment for Bangladesh missionaries on furlough is relearning how to drink water directly from a tap.

We replaced our fragile bamboo outhouse with an inside toilet and septic tank. Of course, we still had to fill the reservoir before each flush, but that was a great improvement. After excavating a huge hole to construct the brick septic tank, the workers were curious to know why I was making an underground "room." They refused to believe when I explained the process of human waste dissolving in a septic tank and dissipating as liquid into the soil. For thousands of years they had made their toilet under banana trees, along the river banks, or in rice fields. No foreigner could improve on that system.

Eleanor's kitchen was a detached bamboo structure, located a few feet behind the main house. In that room Edris, a cook-helper we had inherited from Gene, helped prepare meals and wash dishes. Curious to see how he did that, Eleanor decided to check. Horrified, she watched as he squatted, gripping each plate deftly between his toes, scrubbing off curry stains with sand and ashes. After swishing the plates in a pail of river water, he dried them with a grimy towel. It was not surprising that she quickly instituted some reforms which, without doubt, spared us from some of the stomach problems suffered by our predecessor.

To make our riverside home even more comfortable, I plastered a layer of cement over the mud floor and whitewashed the interior bamboo walls. Each improvement made our situation more livable and enjoyable. Reflecting on those days at Hebron, I must praise Eleanor for the great person she is. How she ever managed to care for the house, for me, and four small children is a miracle.

Life at Hebron was a sink-or-swim situation and this novice missionary, hardly dry behind the ears, had his hands full as did his patient wife. I often tell people that when we married, I promised Eleanor to go with her through all the difficult spots of life. She reminds me that I haven't missed a one.

The Hebron building schedule called for the completion of a missionary residence that Gene had nearly finished, and the construction of a new home for Mary Lou and Joyce Ann. They

wanted their home to look like the tribal houses, built high off
the ground on spidery legs of teak wood and bamboo. I faced those
projects with fear and trembling because my only experience as a
carpenter had been helping a Michigan friend remodel his home.
But I boldly accepted the challenges, trusting the Lord for daily
wisdom.

Joyce Ann and Mary Lou's house was to be 36 feet wide, 60 feet
long and at least four feet off the ground. So I constructed four-
foot high cement pillars, each 12 feet apart. On top of these we
bolted wooden timbers in all directions. We then nailed floor
boards across the timbers. After the floor boards had cured, we
poured a three-inch cement cap over them. I'm sure the Tipperahs
who were helping me wondered about my sanity.

The project went fairly well until it came to figuring out how to
erect the superstructure. One afternoon as I was puzzling over that
problem, Mary Lou handed me a *Better Homes and Gardens* which
she thought might be of help. I could hardly believe my eyes as I
leafed through it. There, in graphic detail, were instructions and
pictures on how to fabricate two-inch by four-inch by eight-inch
stud walls, raise them into upright positions, and tie the building
together with roof trusses. That magazine was a godsend. The Lord
had wonderfully met an urgent, timely need. Little did I realize
then how much I would be involved in either building or super-
vising building projects in future years.

Mary Lou's clinic, a popular feature of the Hebron work, provided medical care for tribal people who trekked in from the hills,
as well as for local Bengali villagers. When she had to be away,
Eleanor took over, especially in an emergency. It seemed as if most
of the emergencies happened during Mary Lou's absences.

Late one evening a boatload of Marma people came with a
pretty teenage girl who, after four days of labor, was unable to
deliver her child. The parents pled with us to get the baby out
before the girl died. Mary Lou was away so Eleanor, though not
feeling well herself (we later learned that she was pregnant with

AGAINST ALL ODDS

A VENTURE OF FAITH WITH THE HILL TRIBES OF BANGLADESH

Author's boyhood home

Below:
Rev. Arthur Glen

Pioneer home missionaries Ralph and
Mabel Hill

"Mr." Hill's car and trailor used to pick up
children for Sunday School

Claude and Minnie Jackson,
who provided a home for Jay

The Walsh family at Hebron, 1960

Above:
Rev. Paul Miller and Rev. Victor Barnard
baptizing a new believer.

Right:
Joyce Ann Wingo with Tipperah students

Jay built this home for Mary Lou and Joyce Ann.

Benu Pandit, the Walshes' language
teacher

A typical Tipperah home

A Tipperah grandmother

The "Pig" Murung

Above:
Jay interviewing Murungs from a distant village.

Left:
Meypong Murung, the first Murung believer

Ancherai, the "Apostle Paul" of the Tipperah people

Pastor Gonachandro Tipperah and his wife. He spent 3 years in jail.

Pastor Gunijon Tipperah, Evangelist Ancherai's protégé

Evangelist Robichandro

twins), took charge. Joyce Ann hurriedly arranged a bed for the patient and Eleanor administered a sedative. We soon discovered that the unborn child had already died and that the girl's uterus had probably ruptured. Determined, the three of us tried to extract the child but were unsuccessful. Physically and emotionally exhausted, we had to tell the hopeful family that there was nothing more we could do. We suggested that they might get help in the distant city of Chittagong, but they decided that going to the city was as impossible as a trip to the moon.

We watched as they gently carried the unconscious girl back to the river. The boat slipped its mooring and they paddled their way upriver to their village home. We knew the girl would die. That terrible experience robbed us of sleep for several nights. Though we had tried our best, we carried lingering guilt because we were unable to help a family that had come with such great expectation and hope. Amazingly, a few days later the girl's father returned bearing the gift of a large rooster. It was his way of expressing appreciation for the efforts we had made to save his daughter and grandchild.

That tragic experience convinced me of the need and importance of medical missions, not only for humanitarian purposes, but also as a tool for evangelism. At about that same time, we had been corresponding with Dr. Viggo B. Olsen, a highly skilled surgeon in the USA, whom the Lord had burdened to establish a medical work in Bangladesh. Five years later, in March 1966, he and a team of medical missionaries dedicated the Memorial Christian Hospital, located 20 miles west of Hebron at a place called Malumghat, not far from the Matamahari River.

THE CASE OF THE MISSING ENGINE

*"Consider it pure joy, my brothers, whenever
you face trials of many kinds, because you
know that the testing of your faith develops
perseverance."*
James 1:2 (NIV)

When Eleanor and I were preparing to go to Bangladesh, we received a letter from Helen Miller requesting that we purchase and take an 18-horsepower Evinrude speedboat engine. "I will pay for it from Paul's memorial fund," she said in her letter. "A speedboat will get us up and down the river more quickly, saving hours of travel time."

She and the Barnards were excited the day we uncrated the engine in Chittagong. Though none of them ever got to use it, Helen donated it to the Hebron station for our use. At first, having a speedboat engine proved to be a mixed blessing because of the effectiveness of the bamboo telegraph (rumors). News that we had an engine spread quickly. Because such modern equipment was still a novelty in remote areas, government officials asked to borrow it for their travel on the river. That posed a problem and I had to find ways to diplomatically refuse, not only because of the engine's value to us, but also because it would set a precedent for the future. If I loaned it to one government official, others, undoubtedly, would expect the same privilege.

One afternoon a military officer asked to borrow the boat, and, as he put it, our "driver." I politely refused on the basis that Michael, our handyman, was still learning how to operate the engine, and that I wanted to get permission from mission headquarters in America. This would take at least a month. Seemingly satisfied with that explanation, he sauntered off.

Several days later, to my horror, I discovered the Evinrude missing from the storage shed. Faced with a major theft, I questioned Michael first, then the night watchman. They knew nothing. I called in the other mission employees one by one. Nobody could supply me with a clue as to who might have taken the engine. Distraught, I hurried one mile across the rice paddies to the Lama Police Station and reported the incident to the Officer in Charge (O.C.). During his inquiry I mentioned the military officer who had wanted to borrow the engine and driver. After the O.C. duly recorded my statements, I returned to Hebron.

The following day two gun-toting soldiers appeared at the door with orders to arrest me. There was nothing I could do but accompany them to their headquarters. As they marched me off, I assured Eleanor that things would be all right and told her not to worry. That, however, was a rather hollow assurance as she was left alone with the children; Mary Lou and Joyce Ann were away in Chittagong. Benu also made an effort to assure her that everything would be fine. He said with a worried expression, "I'll follow to see what happens."

Monsoon rain drenched us as we walked across the slippery rice paddies to the military headquarters in Lama. I was ushered into the presence of a tough-looking colonel who glared at me and sternly asked why I had implicated a military officer in the engine case.

"I didn't, Sir," I replied, "I merely responded to the O.C.'s questions. He asked if I had noticed any strangers around the compound. The only person I could remember was the military officer who had asked to borrow our boat and engine."

The colonel continued to badger me on this point until finally, in disgust, I told him I would make no further statements unless they could be made at the U.S. Embassy in Dhaka. (During the interrogation it popped into my mind that East Pakistan was almost totally dependent on American aid to keep its economy afloat. I would try using political pressure.)

"Let's go to Dhaka," I said boldly. "I'm ready to go now!"

When I mentioned the U.S. Embassy, he backed off and dismissed me. I returned to Hebron without my escorts, except for Benu who had been watching and waiting a short distance away. He had "protected" me, as he proudly told others later.

Another week passed before the O.C. arrived with a contingent of subordinates to investigate the case. I was unaware of their tactics until someone reported that the police were beating up mission employees in their efforts to find the thief. I rushed over to the bamboo hut where their interrogations were being held, and pled with them to stop using such inhumane treatment. The O.C. scowled at me and said, "I am about to solve this case and recover your engine. You wait and see."

It was obvious that he believed the theft had to be an inside job. That's why he had severely beaten Michael, as well as several tribal men, including our Tipperah evangelist, Ancherai. All of them were squatting on the mud floor in front of him, bloody welts covering their backs.

"Let's go," he ordered, striking Michael another stinging blow with his swagger stick. Michael rose and led us to a secluded spot in the nearby jungle where he had buried the engine.

"We know our people," the O.C. lectured me, "and we know how to deal with them." Indeed they did!

During our early days at Hebron, Eleanor and I learned more about missionary work than Missions 101 & 102 ever taught us in Bible school. In fact, there seemed to be little correlation between the textbooks and real life. Take the flood as an example. We were unprepared for that event. We were now living in the house Gene had been building before he left. This, too, was on the riverbank but situated farther back and at a higher level. That July the annual monsoon rains fell with a vengeance. It rained day and night for two weeks. We began to appreciate how the people of Noah's day must have felt at the time of the Great Flood.

The Matamahari River, which usually flows in a channel some 30 feet below its bank, had risen to within one foot of cresting. We missionaries watched anxiously as debris, including huge trees and drowned animals, rushed past in the turbulent currents. Should we pack up our house and move to higher ground? I decided to seek the counsel of the elders in the Buddhist village adjoining our mission property. Had they ever known the river to overflow its banks? To a man they swore it had never happened in their lifetime and some of them were in their seventies.

While I appreciated their input, I returned to find that the river had swollen even more and was beginning to overflow its banks! Fearing the worst, because the skies were still black and heavy, Eleanor and I hurriedly packed our possessions, storing some of them in metal barrels. The rest we stacked on tables inside the house. Then, locking the doors and posting a watchman on the front verandah, we and the children moved in with Mary Lou and Joyce Ann. Their house was located at a safe elevation about a football field-length away. That was one of the longest nights of our missionary experience. Near midnight, still worried about our house, I lit a hurricane lantern and headed down the trail to check things out. No sooner had I started when a poisonous snake, a yellow-banded krait, slithered across the trail near my feet. In fright I dropped the lantern and had to re-light it.

Wading at times through chest-deep water, I reached the house to find the guard curled up in a sound sleep. The muddy flood waters were about to enter the house only inches from his body. After jogging him awake and scolding him for sleeping, which he vigorously denied, I returned to Eleanor, relieved that our possessions were still safe.

Sleep eluded us the rest of that night as torrential rains continued to hammer on the tin roof above us. With the dawning of a new day, the rains slackened to a sprinkle. I rose before the others, eager to check the house again. Before leaving, I paused to read the Word and commit the day to God. Psalm 46 caught my attention, and I was astounded to find in that passage exactly what we had been living through. The waters were indeed roaring and swelling. The mountains and earth (the silt and the foliage) were being carried out to the sea. Things were in an uproar. But, as I read on, I was greatly comforted. I read of a quieter, more gentle river:

> "There is a river, the streams whereof shall make glad the city of God, the holy place of the tabernacles of the most High. God is in the midst of her: she shall not be moved: God shall help her, and that right early" (Psalm 46:4).

And later in the chapter,

> "Be still, and know that I am God: I will be exalted among the heathen. I will be exalted in the earth. The Lord of hosts is with us; the God of Jacob is our refuge. Selah" (Psalm 46:10,11).

As I emerged from our temporary shelter I found that our property, and many areas around the local Buddhist village, were totally inundated. An immense lake now merged with the rampaging river. Only the rooftops of the bamboo huts on both banks could be seen. That huge, muddy lake covered most of our property, including the path leading to our house. The guard, having had a good night's sleep, picked me up in a canoe and skillfully poled me back home. He nosed the boat into the main doorway of the house, now filled with three feet of muddy water.

Later that day when the waters receded, we began the messy cleanup. Someone once defined a mess as two quarts of honey in a one-quart jar. Our mess was comparable. A few kind villagers helped us scrape out the muddy silt that had been deposited on the floor. The goods we had piled on tables were all fine. However, several barrels containing our clothing had buoyed up and tilted, allowing muddy water to seep in. It took Eleanor nearly a week

using a hand-operated washer and wringer to wash, clean, dry, and
repack all those clothes.

Some days later, after scrubbing and cleaning the house, we celebrated by inviting Benu, our teacher, and Khoka, our resident
Bengali evangelist, to have supper with us. Eleanor had prepared
a jello dessert, not realizing that the local people had no equiva-
lent. Khoka, who had enjoyed a tasty feast of rice and curry, gingerly put a spoonful of jello into his mouth and immediately
spewed it out across the room. That slippery, smooth feeling
repulsed him. A bit later, however, he let us know how much he
appreciated the meal by creating an enormous, well-formed belch!
(We learned later that a good belch was one way of compliment-
ing the cook for the meal).

After dinner Khoka presented Eleanor with a gift: a pair of
"twin" bananas (joined like Siamese twins). Making the presenta-
tion, he predicted that she would give birth to twins. In Bengali
folklore if the father of twins gives twin bananas to a pregnant
woman, she will also have twins. We enjoyed a good laugh and
parted ways.

As the summer of 1961 ended, a pregnant Eleanor was miserable and abnormally large. After doing a self-examination she
thought she could feel two heads. Until now she had been counting on nurse Mary Lou to do a home delivery at Hebron. However,
the possibility that she might be carrying twins prompted us to
move to Chittagong. Dr. Makuda, a Japanese doctor living there
at the time, confirmed Eleanor's suspicion and advised us to find a
good hospital since the delivery might be complicated or the
babies born prematurely.

Once again Eleanor and I made the long air journey across
India to Lahore, West Pakistan where she gave birth to our lovely
twin daughters, Sheryl Ann and Shelley Lou, named after our colleagues Joyce Ann Wingo and Mary Lou Brownell. The twins,
born November 13, 1961, were not identical. The next day I
recorded in my journal: "I went at 8:00 a.m. to visit Eleanor, but

before I reached her room Dr. Martin intercepted me and informed me that I was the father of two lovely daughters! I cried."

After we returned to Chittagong with the twins, Lynn Silvernale, Donna Ahlgrim, and the Dr. Vic Olsen family arrived from the USA to join our fledgling missionary team. We had been eagerly looking forward to their arrival and were excited about having their help in the ministries at Hebron and Chittagong. We housed the Olsen family, little realizing how providential that would be.

Sheryl had diarrhea off and on since birth. We changed her formula several times in an effort to solve the problem. She did quite well on the Pet milk that Lynn and Donna brought with them from America, but that soon ran out. In our busyness helping the new missionaries, we failed to detect that this bout of diarrhea was more serious than previous occasions, and that Sheryl was dehydrating. Concerned, we asked Dr Olsen to check her. "Sheryl is very ill," he said with urgency. "We must get her to a hospital immediately."

We decided to take her to the Arthington Memorial Hospital in Chandraghona, about 40 miles away, where several British medical missionaries worked. I hurried to borrow a vehicle, but by the time I returned Vic determined time was running out for Sheryl. She would not survive a two-hour ride to Chandraghona over rough roads. We had to go directly to the nearby government-run Chittagong Medical College Hospital.

Fear surged through us as Dr. Olsen and nurse Mary Lou carried our baby into the emergency room. With considerable difficulty he convinced the student doctors, who thought we were making too much fuss over a two-month-old baby girl, that an IV procedure was necessary. Eventually they cooperated by bringing to him the necessary instruments, none of which had been properly sterilized!

Unable to insert a needle into Sheryl's collasped leg vein, Dr. Olsen started again in her groin. As the second procedure got underway, with Mary Lou shooing away the flies, he asked Eleanor and me to leave. Those were sobering moments as we walked to the parking lot and climbed into the Jeep to think and pray. Both of us faced the dreaded possibility that Sheryl would not survive.

During those moments I prayed audibly for Vic and Mary Lou, committing them to the Lord. Then I told the Lord that we wanted His perfect will to be done, and were ready to accept whatever happened. No sooner had we finished praying than the peace of God flooded our beings. An indescribable peace replaced the fear. We were ready for whatever news would come.

As we stepped out of the Jeep and stood waiting for Vic's call, a man exited the hospital. Walking past us he said in Bengali, "*Hoieche*" (It's over.) That one word carried two diverse meanings: "The operation is over and the baby is dead" or "The operation is over and was successful."

We hurried to the emergency room, peeked through a curtain, and saw the IV fluid dripping life into Sheryl's little body. Vic had saved our baby, his very first patient in the country!

Hebron was not only a proving ground for us young missionaries, it was also the birthplace of three great ministries. Helen Miller had begun a medical work on the verandah of her riverside home. Mary Lou developed that ministry, first from her verandah, and later in a dispensary I built for her. She often attended inpatients as well as scheduling regular days for outpatient service. In field discussions regarding the location of a future full-fledged hospital, we missionaries felt that it must be accessible to the tribal people, especially those living in the Matamahari River valley. Our suggestion was that it be located near Cheringa at the juncture of the Matamahari River and the Arakan Road. Eventually that is where it was built and where tribal patients are now referred.

The literature ministry also had its roots in Hebron. It began with a challenge from Gladys McLean, a visiting missionary from India. After I expressed my interest in finding a way to minister to

English speaking government officials, she challenged me to start a personal literature ministry, similar to what she was doing in India with great success. When she met English-speaking officials and business people, she asked if they would like to receive Christian magazines and literature. With their approval she recorded their names and addresses, later sending them monthly mailings.

After Gladys left Hebron, I began to assemble my own list of personal contacts and mailed them copies of anything I could get my hands on, including Sunday school papers such as Scripture Press's *Power*. Later, to meet the growing need, a laymen's group in Michigan shipped us a regular supply of Christian literature. My list of contacts eventually grew to more than 100 names. When Gene Gurganus returned in January 1962, we rented an apartment on Buddhist Temple Road in Chittagong. Together we set up a reading library of Christian books, an office for dealing with inquirers, and a literature room for the mailing ministry. That simple effort was the humble beginning for a vision yet to be realized.

Jeannie Lockerbie, who inherited writing talents from her author mother, Jeanette Lockerbie Johnston, caught the real literature vision for our mission. Under her leadership the literature ministry grew to be the largest producer of Christian literature in the Bengali language. Today we have our own computers, laser printers, and offset printing presses. Over the years the Bible Literature Center staff has produced millions of tracts, booklets, books, Sunday School curriculum, and AWANA material. The literature ministry continues to impact the growing church in Bangladesh.

The third great ministry to evolve out of Hebron was the tribal work. Hebron today continues to be a center for tribal evangelism and education. Eleanor and I had dedicated our lives to penetrating the tribes with the gospel message. In succeeding years most of our efforts were directed towards reaching the tribe known as the Tipperahs.

CHAPTER 9

OLD PEOPLE HAVE HARD TONGUES

Then Moses said to the Lord, "Please, Lord,
I have never been eloquent, neither recently
nor in time past, nor since Thou hast spoken
to Thy servant: for I am slow of tongue."
And the Lord said to him, "Who has made
man's mouth: Or who makes him dumb or
deaf, or seeing or blind? Is it not I, the Lord?
Now then go, and I, even I, will be with your
mouth, and teach you what you are to say."
Exodus 4:10–12

"Cross-cultural communication" is modern jargon for what, to Eleanor and me in 1960, meant learning the language fluently. For a career missionary there is no acceptable substitute. I have heard less motivated missionaries say that showing love is more important than learning the language. We dare not underestimate the language of love, but that alone will prove woefully inadequate in the long run. Effective cross-cultural communication requires both love and fluency in speaking if one hopes for any measure of success.

Living at Hebron, Eleanor and I were confronted head-on with the awesome language problem. We not only heard the Bengali language and a dialect called Chittagonian, but also the languages of the Tipperah, Marma, and Murung tribes. Our first task was to learn Bengali, the main language of Bangladesh.

Conquering any language involves learning a vocabulary, analyzing the grammar, and mimicking local usage to eliminate a foreign accent. It also involves learning the meanings of unwritten sounds such as "ugh", and body language, such as scolding a child with the eyes which is common among Tipperah women. Next to living a Spirit-controlled life, learning to communicate fluently is the most important task of a career missionary. Eleanor and I have often reminded churches back home that the most crucial time to pray for their missionaries is while they are in language study. Our great enemy, Satan, does not want us to become fluent in our adopted language. If we settle for less than fluency, we become verbal cripples, making us less effective in our work. Sadly, many missionaries have become first-term casualties because they failed to learn the language.

Most missionaries have at one time or another made serious linguistic and cultural mistakes. How can I forget the time I was teaching a lesson about Nicodemus from John chapter three? I explained in Bengali that Nicodemus came to Jesus at night and said, "Rabbi, we know you are a *goru* who has come from God." To my embarrassment the class began to laugh, then corrected me. "*Goru*," they said, "means cow. You should have used *guru* which means teacher." In spite of our mistakes, we found that the nationals are gracious, forgiving and understanding when they see our genuine desire to learn their language and to live lives motivated by the love of Christ. A successful communicator not only learns the language, but takes time to observe and understand local customs. When he does, his effectiveness as an ambassador for Christ is greatly enhanced.

From the moment I set foot in Bangladesh I was determined to learn the language. Like my father before me, I had been raised to be a sociable, friendly, outgoing person. Dad had often said to me,

"Just remember, Son, a smile and a handshake will take you a long way in life." Excellent advice for those of us who wish to learn a foreign language.

The day we opened our barrels and crates in Chittagong, a group of curious children gathered to watch the activity. I had been told that one of the best ways to learn a language was to talk with children. Now this unpacking gave me my first opportunity. To get started I asked Rev. Barnard how to say "What is this?" in Bengali. He replied, "*A-ta ki?*" After carefully rehearsing those strange sounds, I proceeded to practice on the kids. Pointing at a tree I carefully parroted those words, "*A-ta ki?*"

They quickly replied, "*Angoul.*" Aha, *angoul* means tree!

After repeating this new word a few times I pointed to a brick lying on the ground and asked the same question. Again they replied, "*Angoul.*"

That's strange, I thought, *but sometimes words have a slight variation in sound which I may have missed.* I asked my question again, this time pointing at a bamboo house. Once more they replied, "*Angoul.*" Then it suddenly dawned on me that they were repeating the word for finger. I had been pointing with my finger each time and asking, "What is this?" Any ninny should understand that, right?

There was no formal language school in Chittagong when we arrived. Eager for Eleanor and me to get moving in the language, our missionary colleagues recommended that we hire a teacher to live and travel with us. Their advice made sense, so we hired Benu, who accompanied our family to Lahore, West Pakistan, and, after Phillip's birth, to Mansehra.

Each morning in Mansehra, Benu and I met for a language class on the verandah of a government rest house overlooking a deep valley with the snow-capped Himalayas as a backdrop. That pastoral setting was certainly conducive to good language learning. Slowly, but surely, I learned a few Bengali words and phrases, even though I had only Benu to practice on. The people of West

Pakistan speak Urdu, not Bengali. There is an obvious disadvantage when what you learn from the books can't be reinforced in the marketplace. It wasn't until we returned to Chittagong that I began making progress in Bengali.

As one might guess, children learn languages more quickly than adults. We found this not only to be true, but humbling. One morning as I was struggling at language study, I peered out the study window to see our six-year-old son, Douglas, talking with a toothless old tribal lady. *Was he actually carrying on an intelligent conversation with her?* I wondered. Curiosity getting the best of me, I called Doug to find out.

"What are you doing, Son?" I asked.

"Talking to the old *ma* (mother)," he replied.

"Really? What did she say?" He proceeded to tell me that she hadn't been feeling well. She had come out of her quarters and was squatting with her back to the sun, hoping to dispel the chills. *Wow,* I thought. *Doug had picked up all that information not having studied the language? It's difficult enough to understand a person with teeth, let alone someone without any.*

My language study was less than the best. When I asked my language teacher why it was so difficult for adults to speak Bengali he said it was because older people have "hard" tongues; children have "soft" tongues. Now I understood! I had tried the pointing approach with some success. I had also tried learning Bengali in Urdu-speaking West Pakistan with minimal success. Now, with my hands full of work at Hebron, I struggled to find time to spend with Benu. To complicate matters, I discovered that the language spoken in the Hebron area was a corrupted form of Bengali, a local dialect known as Chittagonian. As our first four-year term in Bangladesh came to a close, I had learned to speak bits and pieces of several languages and dialects including those of the Tipperahs, Marmas, and Murungs. But my original goal to conquer "pure" Bengali wasn't fully realized until we returned from our first furlough.

A study tip from Rev. Barnard helped me most in learning the language. He advised me to purchase a few simple Bengali children's books and to read them out loud over and over again, carefully pronouncing each word. Returning to Bangladesh for a second term of service, I had plenty of time to study on board the *Hellenic Leader,* a sister ship to the *Hellenic Splendor.* Each day I practiced reading aloud simple Bible stories about the life of Christ. Those exercises helped me to recognize and pronounce the Bengali sounds more accurately, as well as increase my vocabulary within the context of the stories. From then on, language learning started to be more fun.

As we returned from furlough, my goal was to learn the Tipperah language. The Tipperahs, numbering approximately 40,000, are one of the smaller tribal groups in Bangladesh. They were the people whom Eleanor and I really wanted to evangelize. At first I wondered if learning a second language was possible. Did my brain have room for two? Or would I get hopelessly confused and be ineffective in both languages? This proved not to be the case. The brain, like a powerful computer, has almost endless storage. I found the Tipperah language so totally different from Bengali that it was rather easy, and enjoyable, to assimilate.

A factor that made learning Tipperah easier than I thought it would be was that I could work at my own pace. Learning the Bengali language, a requirement of the mission, monitored by the Language Committee, created a certain amount of mental pressure. I learned Bengali because I *had* to learn it; I tackled the Tipperah language because I *wanted* to. That made a difference.

Tipperah is totally different from Bengali both in grammar and structure. This became painfully apparent when I was learning to count. A Bengali counts from one to five saying *ek, dui, teen, char,* and *panch.* In Tipperah the words are *kaiha, kainui, kaitha, kaibrui* and *kaiba.* One day, as I was practicing Tipperah, I spotted some village pigs and began counting them in the words beginning with "k" as above. "Oh, no!" exclaimed my tutor, "You count pigs like this: *maha, manui, matha, mabrui* and *maba.*" I was frustrated with him. Had he not taught me correctly? Armed with this new information I started counting some children playing nearby. "Oh, no," he scolded again, "You don't count people like pigs. People are counted as *krokha, kroknui, kroktha, krokbrui* and *krokba.*" Only then did I discover that the Tipperahs attach a different generic prefix for each category of things they count.

Learning both the Bengali and Tipperah languages has been enjoyable and educational. Time and again I have been impressed at how extensive and complete is each dialect of even the smallest tribal group. God, who confused languages at Babel, also made each one totally complete and sufficient in itself.

CHAPTER 10

CHANGES A LITTLE WAR CAUSED

"Yea, and all that will live godly in Christ Jesus shall suffer persecution."
2 Timothy 3:12

If experience begets wisdom and maturity, then we returned from our first furlough with a head start. By that time we had seven children, Diane Janine having been born while we were on furlough. Seven was a full quiver for us. Scottish Dr. Martin's advice at the time of Phillip's birth had finally gotten through! We now had the perfect number, and a solution to the problem of who would get the extra dessert on their assigned day of the week.

When we returned from furlough in June of 1965, the field council decided that we should move to the hospital which was under construction at Malumghat, 65 miles south of Chittagong. From there we would continue our tribal ministry. Malumghat, a Bengali word meaning "port of learning", is located in a national virgin forest and borders a tidal canal which wound its way, in the early days, through seven miles of mangrove swamps to the Bay of Bengal. The border of the Chittagong Hill Tracts lies only two miles east of the hospital.

Malumghat was an ideal location for the hospital. The Arakan Road passes in front, giving access to vehicular traffic moving north and south. The canal at the back of the property provides access for patients arriving by boat from the offshore islands and coastal areas. Logging trails penetrating the Hill Tracts to the east make travel convenient for the tribal people also.

By the time we arrived, Memorial Christian Hospital was in the final stages of construction. Building contractor Tom McDonald and his wife, Olline, had requested us to help finish the project which they had taken over from Paul Goodman, the original contractor. We have only praise for Paul Goodman who initiated the project, and the McDonalds, who invested three years of their lives to build a hospital in the midst of an animal-infested jungle. Their faithfulness in the work, and their sterling testimonies, resulted in thousands of Bengali and tribal people hearing the message of Christ's love. Tom and Olline, working against many odds, stayed until the hospital was dedicated on March 26, 1966.

Before Eleanor and I moved to the hospital, Tom sent a messenger requesting us to bring an extra Bengali Bible. It was, he explained, for a man who had recently professed Jesus as his Savior and Lord. We honored his request and after we moved to Malumghat, Tom introduced me to a young man named Syeed-ul-Haq who was working as a guard at the construction site. Tom had already briefed me as to how Syeed had become a believer.

Eager to hear his story, I arranged to meet with Syeed. Spotting the new Bible in my hand, his eyes brightened and a smile of gratitude flashed over his face. When I told him it would cost 10 *takas* (about $2.00 at that time and representing two day's wages), he replied, "I don't care if it costs 100 *takas*, I want my own Bible!"

Insisting that Syeed pay for the Bible was important. Nationals desiring Christian literature must pay something, however little, lest we be accused by the government of "buying Christians." A common though false criticism against missionaries is that they win converts by giving incentives, such as jobs, land, or money.

Syeed opened his heart to me. He had been born on the island of Kutubdia, located a half-mile off the coast in the Bay of Bengal.

He lived there with his wife and two daughters. In 1963 a cyclonic storm made a direct hit on the island, drowning many people in a tidal surge. With sea water rising around their feet, Syeed and his family scrambled to climb a mango tree near their hut. They clung tenaciously to its branches to wait out the storm. At dawn, after the storm had passed, Syeed heard a bird sweetly chirping in the tree near him.

"*Sahib,*" he said, "When I heard that bird singing, I felt at that moment that *Allah* (God) had spared me and my family for a special reason."

Shortly after the cyclone, Syeed moved his family to the mainland near his wife's relatives where they would be safer. He reasoned correctly that there would be more cyclones in the future. His new home turned out to be only a few hundred yards from where Memorial Christian Hospital would be built. Later that year, when construction got underway, Syeed sought work as a day laborer. Tom, impressed with his demeanor, hired Syeed to guard the building materials stashed around the construction site.

For Christmas that year Tom and Olline McDonald presented a new Bible to their Buddhist cook, Monindra. When Syeed made his nightly rounds he peered through the bamboo slats to watch Monindra reading from that mysterious Christian holy book. Curiosity getting the best of him, he asked Monindra if he could read it too. The cook refused. That was *his* special Bible. His *boro sahib* (boss) had given it to him.

The cook's attitude did not deter Syeed. One afternoon while Monindra was working, he pried open the door and borrowed that Bible. After secretly reading random portions, he returned it to its place before the cook came off duty. Syeed kept up this routine for several days, totally spellbound with what he read.

One afternoon Syeed slipped away to a secluded spot and began reading again, this time in Matthew chapter 24. As he read intently about the second coming of Christ, the Holy Spirit over-

powered him and he fell to his knees and called out to Jesus for salvation. At that moment Syeed was gloriously transformed. Syeed
became the first believer at Malumghat.

With his own Bible now in hand, he began to grow in his new
found faith, but couldn't get enough of God's Word. One evening,
after hearing that I was planning to conduct a tribal Bible school
on the hospital compound, Syeed asked permission to attend.
That annual event was designed to provide special Bible training
for tribal pastors and evangelists. Syeed, though not an ethnic
tribal person, was eager to learn more. I couldn't turn him down.

The studies for that week were from the Old Testament book of
Daniel. When the seminar was over, Syeed took me aside and
asked if he could change his name. Surprised, I explained that it
wasn't necessary, but that I had no opposition to the idea.

"What name would you like?" I asked curiously.

"Daniel," he replied. "I want to be like him."

From that moment forward Syeed-ul-Haq became Daniel Haq.
In the months and years to follow, Daniel endured trials and per-
secutions, perhaps even more severe than those of his namesake.

One afternoon the ambulance driver rushed up with the news
that a crowd was beating Daniel in the local bazaar. On hearing
that report, Dr. Olsen rushed to the bazaar where he found Daniel
lying unconscious in a ditch. As he approached the scene, a crowd
of angry young men who had wanted to sever Daniel's tongue
cowardly backed away.

Daniel was admitted to the hospital where he made a good
recovery. He later testified that his enemies had seized and
mocked him. They took turns spitting and urinating on him
before beating him senseless. Many years later in 1992, angry enemies burned his home. The last chapter in Daniel's story has yet
to be written, but the first chapter began when the McDonalds
took time in the midst of a hectic building schedule to arrange for
a man's spiritual needs to be met.

The McDonalds and their 21-year-old son, Fenton, needed a much deserved vacation. Eleanor and I, now settled at the hospital, made that possible. They booked passage on the M.V. *Rustom*, the pride of Pakistan's merchant fleet. Their trip was scheduled to take them from Chittagong to Colombo (Sri Lanka) to Karachi (West Pakistan) and back, all in ten days.

Eleanor and I were now alone at the hospital, facing the task of overseeing the ongoing building project in addition to the tribal ministry. I was quite fearful of this new responsibility. The one encouraging thing in my favor—perhaps the only thing—was that I spoke the language fluently. With the Lord's help I would manage.

Almost everything adverse that could happen to us during the McDonald's absence did happen. Daily temperatures hovered in the high 90's with humidity in the same range. Our children broke out with miserable heat rashes, often resulting in ugly sores. Electricity to run the fans would have helped, but we had none.

Then I was afflicted with huge, bleeding abscesses. They appeared first on my neck, then on my bottom. For the first time in my life I could appreciate Job's predicament. I could neither turn my head nor sit on a chair. That made overseeing the construction project very difficult.

The dense forest around the hospital, covered with thorny underbrush, provided a home for jackals, civet cats, wild boar, barking deer, leopards, elephants, and tigers. Snakes also dwelt there. One evening, while the McDonalds were away, a huge yellow-banded krait slithered up on the verandah. I quickly grabbed my shotgun, hoping to turn it away, if not to kill it. Seeing me and sensing danger, the snake took refuge in a woodpile in front of the house. Sinc the sun had already set, I flashed a light into the woodpile. Spotting a portion of the snake, I squeezed the trigger and waited. Strangely, the snake did not come out.

The next morning, curious to know why, I engaged laborers to dismantle the pile while I stood guard with a loaded gun. Before long they uncovered the six-foot long reptile, long since dead. I had shot off the tail section which, apparently, was enough to do the trick.

On another occasion we were awakened in the dead of night by banging on the door. An old gentleman with a wispy, white beard had come from the nearby village and pled with me to shoot a huge snake that had entered "his house." He clasped his hands and stretched out his arms to form a big oval indicating the snake's size. *Wow,* I thought, *a mammoth python!* Aware of the value of a python skin, I hurriedly dressed, loaded my faithful 12-gauge with fine shot, and gingerly followed my guide.

We approached his house with my flashlight blazing and my gun hoisted for action. Suddenly the old gentleman stopped to warn me that we were near. Inching forward ever so slowly, we came to a lean-to attached to his mud house.

"In there," he whispered, "the snake's in there." Crouching down, I shined my light into his chicken coup. Sure enough, a snake gripped a struggling chicken by the neck, slowly sucking its life blood. I lifted the gun, aimed, and fired. When the dust cleared, I not only had killed the snake but also collapsed the chicken house! The snake, as it turned out to my disappointment, was only a five-foot black cobra. Pleased that I had killed it, the old gentleman offered me the dead chicken as a reward!

"Thanks," I said, "but you're a poor man and you should have it."

I later came to understand that "in my house" meant the entire area within a fenced compound.

While the McDonalds were still away, a 17-day war broke out between India and Pakistan, delaying their return by one month. The Indian Air Force attacked Chittagong's airfield and port areas, dropping several bombs which we heard exploding in the distance. We wondered what would happen next.

As it turned out, that brief war had a lasting effect on the tribal work. After hostilities ended, the Pakistan government began training young men in the Chittagong Hill Tracts to prepare for guerrilla warfare against India. That decision resulted in a policy prohibiting foreign nationals from traveling in the hills. Officials explained to me that their decision was for our protection, but in actuality, the government did not want foreigners snooping into their nefarious activities. Sadly, the policy instituted in 1965 is still in effect today. Without special permission from the Home Ministry, foreigners cannot travel in the tribal hills.

That 1965 skirmish forced ABWE to take a different course in the tribal work. Since we could no longer go to the tribal people, they would have to come to us for fellowship and training, either at Hebron or Malumghat. In time, it also seemed wise to base our tribal missionaries at Malumghat rather than Hebron which is surrounded by the Hill Tracts. We would, however, continue to make periodic visits to Hebron to encourage the national believers and attend their special events.

Over the years the tribal complex at Malumghat expanded to include several residences for evangelists, a large guest house, a hospice for tribal medical patients, an office complex, and a spacious meeting hall. The national chairman of the Tribal Association of Baptist Churches oversees the expanding tribal ministries today from that location.

Moving to Malumghat in 1965 marked the beginning of more than 20 event-filled years. Tribal evangelism, as well as field administrative duties, occupied most of my time. Eleanor was primarily responsible for the family, and for hospitality for the hundreds of people who found their way to our remote corner of the earth. We and our children will forever cherish those wonderful years of serving the Lord in that special place.

CHAPTER 11

THE GREAT WHITE HUNTER

"But meat commendeth us not to God: for nei-
ther, if we eat, are we the better; if we eat not,
are we the worse."
1 Corinthians 8:8

The tribal people of Bangladesh are good hunters. Of necessity, they kill to eat. When they learned that I was also fond of hunting, they appeared often with luring prospects of game. In my home in Michigan's Upper Peninsula, we commonly ate partridge, rabbit, and venison. I had learned to hunt, not simply for sport, but to put meat on the table. As a conservationist, however, I informed the tribals that I would shoot only what they would eat. Trekking through dense jungles, I shot plenty of game for them including bats, lizards, snakes, and monkeys. That seemed like a good policy until I learned that they fed me those same creatures when we reached their villages! That is when I became more selective in my shooting.

One afternoon while I was riding in a dugout canoe with a group of Murungs, they began frantically pointing at a huge tree overhanging the river. A troop of monkeys were foraging among its branches.

"*Maro! Maro!* (Shoot! Shoot!)," they begged.

"No," I said, "monkeys aren't good to eat." Because the Murungs insisted, I took aim and shot one. When it fell into the

river, the Murungs, as excited as kids on a water slide, jumped in
to retrieve their prize. Later that evening I walked over to their
hut for a visit. The men were sitting on their haunches around a
fire waiting for the monkey meat, neatly skewered on bamboo, to
cook. At each end of the skewer, as if holding the rest of the meat
in place, were the monkey's feet. Monkey curry was never one of
my favorites.

On another occasion several Murung tribal men called me to
the river's edge where they had spotted a tree full of hanging fruit
bats.

"Shoot them, *Sahib*," they begged. "They make delicious curry."

Inserting several rounds of bird shot into my trusty shotgun, and
positioning myself at a distance that would get the best results, I
squeezed off a couple of rounds. Dozens of bats fell into the water
while others took flight. There were bats everywhere. When my
tribal friends retrieved the dead and wounded, they proudly
offered them to me. I knew this was just a courteous gesture, for
which I was thankful. I politely turned them down saying that my
supper had already been prepared. They walked away pleased with
their haul. I too walked away pleased with *their* haul.

The jungles of Bangladesh abound with wild pigs, a constant
menace to the tribal people because they destroy so much of the
annual rice crop. But in a predominantly Muslim country, pigs are
seldom mentioned. Muslims, like Jews, consider pigs filthy and
disgusting, not to be tolerated. I saw this clearly on one occasion
when I attended a diplomatic function in Dhaka, the capital of
Bangladesh. There I met a Canadian who was studying the eco-
nomic problems of the tribal peoples living in the Chittagong Hill
Tracts. During our conversation he proudly stated, "I have produced an eight-volume study on the subject."

My interest aroused, I asked him what his research had shown
about how much of the tribal annual rice crop was destroyed by
wild pigs. He looked at me with a puzzled expression and said, "I
have nothing in my report about wild pigs."

Taking him aside from his Bangladeshi guide and informant, I explained that my records showed approximately 25 percent of the annual crop is lost to foraging wild pigs. I also suggested that one of the best solutions for solving that problem and thereby improving the tribal economy would be to provide every village headman with a shotgun and ammunition. The villagers could shoot the pigs for meat, while, at the same time, saving their rice. I had already done this for two Tipperah villages with good success.

My friend, obviously upset by the information, glanced in the direction of his guide and interpreter, saying, "I can't believe this. How is it that he never told me about wild pigs?"

"Don't be too upset with him," I explained. " You must remember that pigs are *haram* (forbidden) to Muslims. In our area of Bangladesh they even avoid using the word by referring to them as *kalo horeen* (black deer)." Excusing himself, he walked across the room to rejoin his friend. I left the party hoping I hadn't completely ruined his evening.

Everyone, including missionaries, needs some kind of hobby or recreation to balance out a busy life. My favorite leisure time activity was hunting wild boar. I thoroughly enjoyed roaming the jungle paths, shotgun in hand, seeking an opportunity to literally bring home the bacon. During the past 30 years I have bagged several hundred of those wild creatures. Hunting not only provided a diversion from my daily work but also put meat on the tables of our non-Muslim national friends and fellow missionaries. Though I never deliberately sought the title, I became the famous "white hunter" of southern Bangladesh.

One evening at dusk, several tribal men and I sneaked along a jungle path in search of wild pigs. We had already seen tracks where they crossed from one side of the trail to the other. Nearing a crossing where, in the past, I had often encountered game, I asked the men to wait quietly some distance behind me to reduce the noise factor. Wild pigs spook easily. I proceeded forward, safety pin off, moving as quietly as a cat after its prey. Suddenly, in the jungle in front of me, I heard the unnatural snap of a twig. Alerted, I stopped, raised the gun to my shoulder, and waited. Ever so cautiously, as I stared in the twilight, a huge boar poked out its head as if to inspect the path for danger. I stood breathless, frozen in my tracks to avoid a tip-off of my presence. Apparently satisfied, the boar stepped into full view. I squeezed the trigger, dropping the tusker in its tracks.

On hearing the shot, my companions rushed to see what had happened. Seeing the huge boar lying sprawled in the pathway, they jumped with excitement. One of the men pulled a machete from his belt and cautiously inched up to the pig to make sure it was dead. It wasn't. On being poked with the machete, the pig made one last lunge in our direction, scaring the tar out of us, then expired. It took four men to carry the animal out of the jungle. We estimated its weight between 250 and 300 pounds.

Missionary Willard Benedict and I will never forget one pig hunting expedition. He and his wife Donna traveled from Hebron, where they lived, to Malumghat to celebrate their wedding anniversary. Earlier that day I had walked across a small rice field full of fresh pig tracks. Wild pigs forage for food after dark, standing rice crops being their favorite meal.

"Willard," I said, "let's go tonight and shoot a wild boar. This afternoon I found a spot where we're sure to have some luck. The pigs should be out between 10:00 and 11:00 p.m."

He thought for a minute and said, "Sure, I'll go, but you'll have to arrange a gun for me." Having lived most of his life in New York City, Willard wasn't an experienced hunter. It would be fun to show him how it was done.

That night, a mile north of the hospital, we entered a jungle trail that led to my special spot. It was pitch dark, but I knew the trails well. As we approached the area, I stopped and whispered to Willard, "We're very close now. Be super quiet. If the pigs hear the slightest noise, they're gone." We inched forward again, step by careful step, until we were near the field. From that distance we would be able to hear the telltale sound of pigs chomping on the rice. I listened.

"Sure enough," I whispered excitedly, "the pigs are in the rice. You stay here with your gun ready. I'll sneak over to the left nearer to the sound. When I'm ready, I'll switch on my flashlight and fire at the first pig I see. You can shoot at the other pigs as they run past you."

Leaving Willard standing alone in the dark, I tiptoed nearer in the direction of the sounds and stopped. Satisfied that I was close enough, I composed myself with a deep breath, lifted the gun to my shoulder and flashed on the light. A huge wild elephant reared back on its haunches, front legs pawing the air, and let out a blood-curdling trumpet. A shot of adrenaline surged through my body!

Wild elephants in Bangladesh are just that—wild. Over the years many injury cases arrived at the hospital. We regularly heard of people killed by rogues. An elephant entered a village near the hospital one night, uprooting and eating banana trees. An unsuspecting villager opened his door to check on the noise. At that moment the elephant, sensing danger, hoisted the man in the air with its trunk, threw him to the ground, and gently stepped on his head.

All this flashed through my mind as I found myself in the dark, facing a wild elephant less than a hundred feet away. Fast thinking was crucial. If it charged me, I would have to fire my gun in self defense. That was the last thing I wanted to do because elephants are a protected species. I kept the gun, loaded with only three rounds of buckshot, aimed at the elephant's head, my flashlight beaming in its eyes. If it charged me I might be able to scare it away with a blast or two. However, when the behemoth dropped on all fours again, instead of charging me, it sauntered away in the opposite direction, apparently afraid of the bright light. Greatly relieved, I backed slowly in Willard's direction, still prepared to shoot should the elephant change its mind. When I reached him he said, "Jay, I think we'd better get out of here." That was the understatement of the day.

"Okay," I agreed, trying to sound nonchalant. "I doubt that any pigs will come here tonight. And besides, it is your wedding anniversary."

Bangladesh is famous for the Royal Bengal tiger. Those beautiful creatures are now protected by law. However, occasionally an old tiger, unable to catch its natural prey of deer and wild pigs, will attack domestic animals. They have also been known to kill humans. With permission from the Conservator of Forests, these old tigers may be shot.

Late one afternoon, a tribal man from the nearby hills told me that a tiger had killed his cow. I had heard reports of other cow killings, so I decided to accompany my friend to inspect the kill which he had covered with a bamboo mat to protect it from the blazing sun. The dead cow lay only 50 feet from his house. There was no doubt it was the work of a tiger. Telltale teeth marks on its neck were proof enough that the big cat had found the jugular.

Since tigers only kill to eat, this one had feasted on a hind quarter before returning to its jungle sanctuary. I knew it would return to eat again that night, so I decided to try my luck.

Arriving at the farmer's house at sunset, ready for action, I carried my shotgun and a brand new, three-cell flashlight. The farmer helped me construct a blind inside the cow shed attached to his house where he had kept his cow before it was killed. Comfortably seated in the straw, I practiced quietly lifting the gun, flashlight in hand, and pointing them in the direction of the dead cow through an opening in the shed wall. This maneuver would have to be done noiselessly if the tiger returned. Satisfied with my preparations, the old gentleman and I enjoyed a plate of curry before he retired for the night. Then I took up my position in the shed.

For nearly two hours I waited in the rice straw, listening to frogs and crickets with the gun on my lap and the flashlight at my side. As the insects droned on in the surrounding trees, I fought sleep.

Suddenly, around 10:00 p.m., I heard a noise like a dog lapping water, "Slurp, slurp, slurp." My mind went into high gear and my heart began to pump as I realized that just 50 feet away a Royal Bengal tiger was dining on dead cow.

I rose silently to a sitting position. Then, after a moment to gain my composure, I lifted my gun and flashlight into position without alerting the tiger while it continued to eat. That's when everything went wrong.

With the gun pointed in the right direction, my new flashlight failed to light. Frantically I pushed the switch back and forth, then pulled it back to make an adjustment. The flashlight worked this time but the tiger was long gone. The *krrik, krrik* sound of my efforts to activate the light was enough to warn the tiger of impending danger. It bounded away.

Still hoping to get a shot, I sprang from the bamboo shed and ran to the dead cow, flashing my light across the rice paddies. Several hundred yards away, and out of gunshot range, I spotted the tiger's blazing eyes looking back at me. I knew then, as did the tiger, that it had outfoxed me.

I wasn't able to hunt again the following night, although I should have. The farmer came back with the news that the tiger did return and dragged the carcass away. No doubt, that lucky "king of the jungle" is still roaming the hills.

On another occasion two men brought news that a tiger was hiding in a cave in the nearby jungle. The tiger had injured a cow but was unsuccessful in killing it. In response to their entreaties I shouldered my gun and accompanied them. Arriving at the scene, I found a large group of men jabbering excitedly and surrounding a tiger they had already killed.

That tiger was a mere cub, which I determined had probably been abandoned by its mother. This is often the case when a tigress gives birth to more than two cubs. Unable to kill enough food for them all, she will abandon one to hunt on its own. This tiger kitten, weak and emaciated, was unable to kill its prey and had taken refuge in the cave. It measured about six feet from nose to extended tail.

After some heated bargaining, I convinced the men to sell me the carcass, which I skinned and sent to Chittagong for tanning. Though small, the skin was beautiful and I was proud to have it. But not for long. On our next furlough we displayed it in the churches. It was snatched off our curio table and never returned. That was the year a certain gasoline company advertised its brand with the slogan, "Put a tiger in your tank!"

CHAPTER 12

THE LUSHAI CONNECTION

*"How beautiful upon the mountains are the feet
of him that bringeth good tidings, that publisheth
peace; that bringeth good tidings of good, that
publisheth salvation; that saith unto Zion, Thy
God reigneth!"*

Isaiah 52:7

While living at Hebron, Eleanor and I found that it was a hub
for tribal contacts and evangelism. Twice weekly, usually on
Tuesdays and Saturdays, tribal people trekked in from the hills to
do their marketing. When it became known that missionaries
were living at Hebron, they passed our way out of curiosity, just to
see us. It was not uncommon throughout the daylight hours to
find people peering at us through the windows or open doors. To
capture our attention, they coughed or spit. We had precious little
privacy until we retired for the night. In this way, however, we
came to know many wonderful people, especially those of the
Tipperah tribe. Eventually, the Tipperahs began to invite us to
their villages.

In January 1962, Gene Gurganus and I made a long, arduous
trip up the Sangu River to Duniram Tipperah Village, deep in the
Chittagong Hill Tracts near the Indian border. We had heard
rumors that the people of that village had previously been exposed

to the gospel. On reaching their village we were astounded to find a rough hewn stone monument on which was inscribed:

THE GOSPEL WAS FIRST PREACHED IN THIS
VILLAGE BY CHALA LUSHAI IN 1958.

On further investigation, we learned that Chala Lushai, a former Indian army officer, left the Indian state of Mizoram after his conversion to Christ to become an itinerant evangelist in the northern areas of the Chittagong Hill Tracts. Through his efforts two Tipperahs named Robichandro and Ancherai first heard about Christ and His power to save. In time, both of these men became vibrant evangelists who worked with me, and other ABWE missionaries, for more than 30 years. They played a major role in evangelizing their own people, as well as the surrounding Murung and Marma tribes.

Robichandro was converted to Christ and baptized by Chala Lushai in 1958. Robi, as we nicknamed him, was born in a Hindu family in the Hill Tracts town of Kaptai. One of nine children, he learned the religion of his parents who sacrificed chickens, goats, or pigs to Hindu deities. Animal sacrifice was essential to please the gods and obtain salvation.

With the opening of the Kaptai Electric Project on the Karnaphuli River, a major watershed of the Chittagong Hill Tracts, thousands of acres of tribal lands were inundated, forcing people to move away. Robi's family moved south and eventually resettled in Duniram Tipperah Village near the Sangu River. Robi was 18 at the time. Two years later his parents arranged his marriage.

About his conversion Robi recalls, "After my marriage to Aroti, a Lushai tribesman named Chala Lushai crossed over the mountains from India with his family. They settled in our village where they lived for three years. Although he couldn't speak our Ushai dialect, he was able to communicate in Riang, another Tipperah dialect which we understood."

Robi continued, "Chala brought with him a Christian hymn book and a Bible in the Lushai language. He preached about Jesus and taught the villagers many hymns. Though I had no thought of changing my religion, many of our villagers did. Twenty families— half of the village—became Christians and were baptized. They also built a 'Jesus House' (church) in the village."

Observing all that was happening, Robi began to worry about his wayward life. Thoughts of death and hell troubled him. He was, however, addicted to rice whiskey, a habit he found difficult to break until he, too, decided to trust Christ.

As he tells it, "One day I went to a pond in the nearby jungle. Alone, I knelt by a tree with my face to the ground and cried out to God for salvation. In that moment I felt a great burden lifted from my heart. I hurried to report this to Chala and two days later he baptized me. I still had liquor in my house but I threw it out and have never touched it since." In time all 40 families in the village became Christians.

After evangelizing Robichandro's village, Chala began preaching forays into the surrounding hills. His itinerary eventually led him to nearby Ruma Tipperah Village, where Robi's uncle, Ancherai, was the headman. Ancherai, like many village leaders in the hills, caroused, accepted bribes, and drank heavily. On hearing Chala's preaching, he became deeply depressed and, as he later revealed, felt a burden on his head "as heavy as a boulder." When Ancherai finally believed the gospel message, the burden fell off. He was so full of joy at having been released from the weight of sin, he felt compelled to go to the surrounding villages and tell his relatives and friends.

Chala and Ancherai, like Paul and Timothy, started preaching tours throughout the Sangu area. The response of the people to the gospel was so overwhelming they decided to look for a mission to help them. Ancherai had heard of a missionary living in Rangamati, capital of the Chittagong Hill Tracts. He went there but was turned away because that mission was understaffed and

had no funds to expand their work. The resident missionary gave
Ancherai a Bible in the Bengali language before sending him
away. Ancherai, though only semi-literate, was thrilled to have his
own Bible. This became his constant companion in following
years.

Fascinating and wonderful was the way God used Chala and the
Lushai people of Mizoram, India to evangelize the tribal people in
Bangladesh. The Lushais—also called Mizos, meaning "people of
the hills"—inhabit the Indian state of Mizoram east of the northern Chittagong Hill Tracts. Once fierce headhunters and warriors,
the Lushais today are reported to be 96% Christian.

Their fame as headhunters became widely known in 1871 when
a group of Lushai warriors attacked a British tea plantation, killing
and beheading Mr. James Winchester, a widower, and kidnapping
his six-year-old daughter, Mary. She lived for more than a year as
a primitive Lushai girl, eating, among other things, dog meat and
monitor lizards. She was eventually rescued by British soldiers
who, after numerous attacks, killed hundreds of Lushais and burned
their villages. Mr. Winchester's death is still commemorated on a
simple gravestone, now overgrown and mildewed, in the tiny
European cemetery in Cachar, Assam:

"IN MEMORY OF JAMES WINCHESTER WHO WAS
KILLED IN A LUSHAI ATTACK IN ALEXANDRAPORE
GARDEN, JANUARY 23, 1871. THIS IS ERECTED BY
THE EUROPEAN INHABITANTS OF CACHAR."

The first Christian missionary to contact the Lushai tribe was a
young Welsh Presbyterian named Rev. W. Williams. He started his
missionary career in 1891 among the Khasi people of Assam,
India. The Khasi tribe live 100 miles north of the Lushai Hills. On
hearing of the Lushais to the south, Rev. Williams decided to
make an exploratory trip. After two weeks of arduous trekking, he
reached the town of Aizawl, the present capital of Mizoram, then
only a major bazaar.

Williams spent a month in Aizawl before returning to his Khasi work. Greatly impressed and challenged, he mailed letters to England telling of his experiences in the Lushai Hills. These were published in a periodical of the Welsh Presbyterian Church. Williams' appeal so captivated the clergy at home that their Assembly officially adopted the Lushai Hills as a mission field. Sadly, several months after returning from his visit to Aizawl, Williams died of typhoid at age 33. It was he, however, who first brought the name of Christ to the Lushai people and the challenge to churches in Wales.

Later, two independent missionaries supported by a wealthy Christian named Robert Arthington of England, took up the Lushai challenge. J. H. Lorrain and F. W. Savidge, who later joined the British Baptist Missionary Society (BMS), settled in Aizawl on January 11, 1889. Those men faithfully preached the gospel to the Lushais until the BMS reassigned them to work in Assam. The Lushai people still celebrate January 11 as the "Day of the Coming of the Gospel to Mizoram." The departure of Lorrain and Savidge from the Lushai Hills again opened the door for the Welsh Presbyterians to enter.

Presbyterian missionary D.E. Jones took up residence in Aizawl in 1897. His goal was to fulfill the vision of his predecessor, Rev. Williams. Jones quickly learned to speak the Lushai language and was able to build on the solid foundation that Lorrain and Savidge had laid. Before leaving, they had completed the compilation of an English/Lushai dictionary and translated portions of the Bible, including Luke, John and Acts.

Jones was alone in the work until late 1898 when he was joined by the Rev. Edwin Rowlands. Rowlands turned out to be an unusually capable linguist, a born teacher, and a hymn writer of exceptional ability. He and Jones traveled and preached throughout the Lushai Hills, winning a number of young men to the Lord. After being trained in the Word, these Lushai evangelists were used mightily by God to reach their own people. Many years later in Bangladesh, we found the same principle of training national evangelists especially effective.

Starting primary schools in the villages was a major factor in the Lushai work. Lorrain and Savidge started a small school in Aizawl to make primary education available. That school was closed for a time after they left. But in February of 1898, after five months of Lushai language study, Mr. Jones celebrated his 28th birthday by re-opening the school. A year later, Rev. Rowlands took it over, emphasizing the simple skills of reading, writing, and hygiene. The opening of the hearts and minds of the youth through literacy proved to be the key for the advance of the gospel among the Lushai.

In 1904, under the influence of Evan Roberts, the great Welsh Revival broke out in England and Wales. Presbyterian missionary, Rev. John Roberts, on furlough at the time, returned to work with the Khasi tribe and brought the Welsh revival spirit with him. Within a year more than 5,000 converts were added to the Khasi church! Hearing this news, the Lushai leaders sent young people to attend the Khasi meetings. Although unable to understand the Khasi language, they were deeply impressed by the singing, and were strangely moved in their own lives by the Spirit of God. On returning home they started village prayer meetings. Soon hundreds of Lushais were turning to Christ.

From that time on, music became important in the evangelization of the Lushai tribe. Baptist Missionary Society missionary Dr. G. O. Teichmann, on a visit to Lungleh, Mizoram, told of a blind man who had composed a religious cantata based on the first eleven verses of Galatians. He divided the whole village into soprano, alto, tenor, and bass groups, and presented an evening of inspirational singing. Lushai villages, like tribal villages in Bangladesh, are perched on the tops of hills. During their worship services, singing voices echo across the hills.

The revivals that swept the Lushai Hills resulted in a brotherly love that was previously unknown. It was said that the miracle in

Mizoram was not simply in numbers. The whole society changed from headhunters to fishers of men; from families where wives were frequently changed, to stable homes where divorce was almost eradicated. A people without a written language became the most literate tribe in all of India. An unreached people became a church whose primary concern in the following decades was to send missionaries to the unbelievers of the surrounding nations.

The Bawm tribe, living adjacent to the Tipperah villages in the northern Chittagong Hill Tracts, was evangelized by the Lushais. And Chala Lushai's preaching to the Tipperah people of the Sangu Valley produced two wonderful evangelists, Ancherai and Robichandro.

The beautiful, harmonic singing of the Sangu Tipperahs always impressed me during annual visits to that area from 1960 to 1965. We learned that Lushai and Bawm Christians taught their advanced hymnology to some of the Sangu Tipperahs. The Sangu Tipperahs then taught the Matamahari Valley Tipperahs at the annual Bible conferences held at Hebron. That love of music, without a doubt, came from Mr. Edwin Rowlands and the Lushai Christians he taught.

INDIA'S MOST WANTED REBEL

*"And ye shall be hated of all men for my name's
sake but he that endureth to the end shall be
saved. But when they persecute you in this city,
flee into another . . ."*
Matthew 10:22–23

My first Lushai contact came in 1966, shortly after the brief
1965 war between Pakistan and India. During that year, the
Lushais of Mizoram rose up in rebellion against the Indian government in an effort to gain political autonomy and rid Mizoram
of Indian military control. Angered, the Indian government
launched a crackdown against the Lushai leaders, many of whom
crossed into the Sangu area of the Chittagong Hill Tracts for
refuge.

One afternoon a man appeared at our hospital asking to see a
missionary. The guard, observing that he was tribal, guided him to
our house. He wore a native *lungie* (a long skirt fastened at the
waist), and looked disheveled and tired. He was, I observed,
unusually fair-skinned and tall for a tribal person, certainly different in appearance from the Tipperahs, Marmas, and Murungs with
whom we worked.

"Can I help you?" I asked in Bengali.

He replied in broken Bengali, "I've made a long journey from

the hills and would like a room for the night. I would also like a
dental appointment for tomorrow, if that is possible. And could I
also have some private time with you?"

After assuring him of my help, I arranged a room in the staff
quarters and asked him to return in the morning.

He appeared the next day, not in a *lungie* but dressed in a suit
and tie. We greeted each other with a *nomaskar,* the usual Bengali
greeting. Then, in perfect English, he asked if we could talk. I
understood then that he must be some kind of dignitary.

Indeed he was. He introduced himself as L.M.S. Colney, a
Lushai   senator,   representing   the   outlawed   "Christian
Government" of Mizoram. I sat for hours, riveted, as he talked
about his people and their efforts to gain independence from
India. He shared how he had come to Christ and mentioned his
great desire to acquire Christian literature for the people of India.
He stated it this way, "In our struggle for independence, guns are
not needed, Bibles are. India can only be changed if she hears the
gospel and turns to Christ. This can only be accomplished through
literature and evangelism."

Inquiring about his "senatorship" I learned that he was a leader
in a rebel movement, a senator of the underground government.
The Indian army, he explained, was forcefully occupying Mizoram.
This angered the Lushai people who were repulsed by idolatrous
Hindus ruling their Christian land.

"We are Christians," he emphasized, "and we want our own
Christian government. It will be a Christocracy."

Mr. Colney further revealed that their political leader was Mr.
Laldenga Lushai, and that the rebels had been allowed refuge in
the Chittagong Hill Tracts because Pakistan was at that time
India's enemy. While hiding in a Christian Tipperah village in the
Sangu Valley area, Mr. Colney learned about the Memorial
Christian Hospital and decided to make contact.

Between 1966 and 1971, Senator Colney and other Lushai
rebels continued to make periodic medical visits to our hospital.

But in December 1971, after East Pakistan became Bangladesh with India's help, the Lushais were no longer welcome or safe. The new government of Bangladesh, with India's prodding, closed the border between Bangladesh and Mizoram, making life difficult for the rebel leaders.

One day in 1972, nearly a year after the birth of Bangladesh, Eleanor and I were visiting our children in high school at Murree, Pakistan. An American missionary from Rawalpindi spoke to us about his neighbors, whom he described as being from Bangladesh. He had told these men that we were in Murree and they were eager to meet us.

We had no idea who the neighbors were, but several days later, a delegation of five well-dressed tribal men appeared at our door. "I'm Laldenga," the spokesman said, "and these are my aides. We are Lushais from Mizoram." Suddenly it dawned on me that Laldenga was the famous rebel leader of Mizoram whose name was at the top of India's most-wanted political criminal list.

Eleanor served tea as we sat on the verandah rehearsing the recent war that had turned East Pakistan into Bangladesh. Laldenga explained that when East Pakistan became Bangladesh, the Lushais lost their refuge in the Chittagong Hill Tracts. He and his aides fled to Rangoon, Burma where they were given political asylum in the Pakistan Embassy. Later they were flown to Rawalpindi as official "guests" of the Pakistan government.

I mentioned to Laldenga my former contacts with Mr. Colney and other Lushais who had occasionally visited our hospital. He knew of those visits. He shared with me his people's struggle for independence and how desperately he wanted to find a way to let Western nations know of their plight. His visit that day was to ask for my help.

"If America and England won't come to our aid," he reasoned, "our only alternative is to turn to China. That would be going against our Christian principles because we don't believe in Communism; however, our freedom is important."

I don't think he believed me when I told him that we missionaries were private citizens, and, as such, had no special influence
with our respective governments. Before leaving that evening,
Laldenga asked if I would mail some important letters for him; I
agreed to do so. Several days later he returned with two letters,
one addressed to the Queen of England, and the other to evangelist Billy Graham.

In 1987, while listening to the English news service of All India
Radio, I was stunned to hear that Mr. Laldenga had been appointed
by the Indian government as the first governor of semi-
autonomous Mizoram. This was the first news I had heard of
Laldenga since that meeting in Murree 15 years earlier. Obviously,
he had come to some kind of political agreement with the government of India. Remembering his invitation to us to visit
Mizoram, I wrote Mr. Laldenga a congratulatory letter in which I
also spoke of our desire to visit. Surprisingly, we received the following message from his private secretary:

"Sir, I am directed by the Hon'able Chief Minister of Mizoram
(Shri Laldenga) to inform you that permission for your visit to
Mizoram with your wife has been moved to the Gov't. of India.
The Home Minister, Gov't. of India, intimated to us that a telex
has been sent to the High Commission of India, Dhaka, to grant
an entry permit to visit Mizoram for seven days.

"Please contact the High Commission of India, Dhaka on the
matter and let us know your program well in advance as desired by
the Chief Minister please."

Unfortunately, due to a continuing sensitive political situation
in the Chittagong Hill Tracts, and the possibility that the
Bangladesh Government might question our motives for a trip to
Mizoram, we never took advantage of that opportunity.
Eventually we learned that Mr. Laldenga, after serving his term as
governor of semi-autonimous Mizoram, lost his seat in a subsequent election.

We often reflect on the way God works among the nations. Revival in England and Wales brought revival to the Khasi people. Revival fires were then ignited in the Lushai Hills which, in turn, spread into northern Burma and Bangladesh. Then, in 1959, ABWE missionaries picked up the torch and, by training Ancherai, Robichandro and others, spread the gospel message to the Tipperah people of the southern Chittagong Hill Tracts, and to the Marma, Murung, and Chakma tribes of Bangladesh.

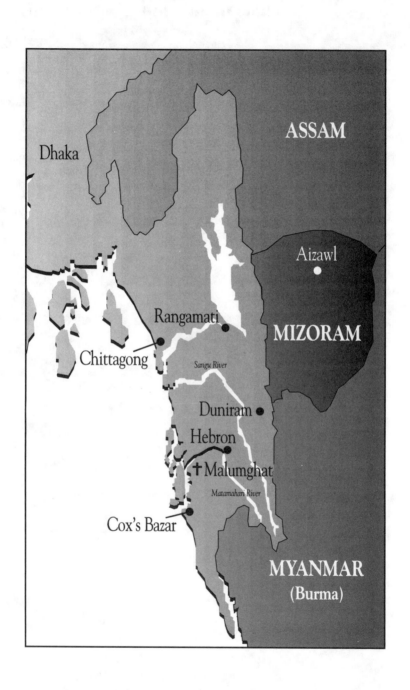

CHAPTER 14

ANCHERAI, "APOSTLE PAUL" OF THE TIPPERAHS

"Paul, a servant of Jesus Christ, called to be an
apostle, seperated unto the gospel of God . . .
for I am not ashamed of the gospel of Christ;
for it is the power of God unto salvation to
everyone that beleiveth."
Romans 1:1,16

In 1959, after learning that the Barnards had opened the Hebron station in the Matamahari River area, Ancherai Tipperah and Chala Lushai sought employment there as itinerant evangelists. Impressed with their testimonies, Rev. Barnard hired them. A year later when Eleanor and I arrived at Hebron, only Ancherai remained. Chala had returned to India.

Ancherai was a man who immediately endeared himself with a congenial spirit and generous smile. Like Rev. Barnard, I recognized the qualities of Christian leadership in this special man of God. The Lord, however, allowed a detour in Ancherai's life that would refine him as gold and turn him into a compassionate evangelist.

During Michael's interrogation by the police over the Evinrude engine theft, out of spite he implicated evangelist Ancherai and a Tipperah night watchman. Because of that allegation, both men were arrested with Michael, beaten, shackled, and taken to the distant seaport town of Cox's Bazar where they were jailed.

Three months later I received a summons to appear in the Cox's Bazar court as a witness at their trial. On arrival I sought out the Officer-in-Charge to brief me on the case. He whispered to me privately that the Tipperahs, in his opinion, had been falsely implicated and that he would try for their early release.

That was wonderful news for us missionaries because we were not sure about Ancherai's involvement. After answering a few questions in court, and giving positive identification to exhibit A (the only Evinrude in the whole of Bangladesh), the judge convicted Michael and released the Tipperahs, who joyfully returned with me to Hebron. Michael was given a two-year jail sentence. Later it came to light that, prior to the theft, he had indeed conspired with the army officer who wanted to borrow the engine.

After being released from jail, Ancherai rejoined his family in the hills. Several weeks later, when he failed to return to Hebron, we began to wonder if he was ill or deliberately avoiding us. During his three months in prison Ancherai's health had deteriorated due to poor and insufficient food. Concerned, I sent word that I needed to talk with him.

Ancherai seemed more subdued, more serious. As we talked together it became clear why he had been avoiding us. The Evinrude engine ordeal had been terribly embarrassing for him. For a man of his character and position to be ignominiously accused, beaten, and marched off in my presence was a humiliation.

But as we talked, Ancherai also admitted that prior to his jail experience he had been living in a backslidden condition, almost as a nominal Christian. He had sought employment from the mission primarily because he needed money. He confessed to cheating the Barnards on bazaar shopping trips, charging them more than he had actually paid for various items. Though I could hardly believe what I was hearing, I sensed that God was doing a special work of grace in Ancherai's heart. Confession was good for his soul.

Speaking to me humbly he said, "*Sahib*, while I was in jail God dealt with me in a very special way. The jail was crowded with prisoners. There was no place to stretch out and sleep so we crouched in a sitting position all night long. Rats infested the place, scurrying among us during the night hours. On several occasions they bit me. Besides that, the other prisoners scorned us because we are tribal people. As minority 'hillies' we were considered inferior and they verbally abused us. Those three months are horrible for me to think about except for one thing."

That "one thing" was the most important that could have happened to Ancherai: he got his heart right with God. He was transformed from a backslidden believer to a dedicated servant of the Lord. One night, crouched in a corner of the filthy jail, Anchari dreamed that an angel appeared in dazzling white garments, assuring him that he was a true child of God and telling him that God wanted him to preach the gospel in the hill country. Ancherai then told me, "*Sahib*, the dream was so real I awoke and started praising the Lord and praying. The peace of God flooded my life and, for the very first time since I was saved, I felt I was really communing with my Lord. I knew He was going to free me so I could preach His Word."

Ancherai rejoined the mission staff and, at his request, was baptized at Hebron. It became my special privilege in the succeeding years to spend many hours teaching him the Word of God. He loved the Word and, being semi-literate, often came to me for explanation and interpretation of those passages he couldn't readily understand. We formed an effective working pattern in our relationship together. After a week or more receiving instruction, Ancherai would head for the hills on a preaching tour. Several weeks later he would return, sharing exciting stories of whole villages turning to Christ and being baptized.

He also shared with me the problems he faced. On one occasion police detained him for a week because he didn't have an identity pass. Ancherai knew the real reason for their action was to stop him from preaching Christ. No law required identity passes.

At other times Ancherai would preach to a group of interested villagers when an opposing group in the same village, drunk with rice whiskey, would deliberately hoot and holler to interrupt his meeting. But, whatever transpired on those preaching trips, Ancherai always returned, eager for more teaching from the Word. Repeating the process, we sat across a table on the verandah, working our way verse by verse through the Scriptures that he longed to understand.

In a tribal committee report of October 1971, I wrote: "This man's hunger for the Word is nothing short of amazing! He pours over his Bible every spare minute. During the past quarter he has come to Malumghat on several occasions for teaching. We have read verse by verse through the gospel of Mark and the book of Revelation. After completing Revelation he commented, "Before when I read this book I could only understand one-tenth of it. Now I can understand seven-tenths." (I didn't tell him that I still understand only about one-tenth.) Ancherai could hardly wait to tell his people about the seven churches of Asia, the seven seals, and the seven angels with the seven plagues!

Occasionally Ancherai would find a verse that captured his curiosity. I recall one morning he came with a question about Proverbs 11:22, "I recognize the words *gold, swine,* and *woman,*" he said, "but what is the meaning?"

"Did you ever see a pretty girl who acted indiscreetly around the opposite sex?" I asked.

"Yes," he replied, "there's one in every village."

"Well," I explained, "she spoils her beauty by the way she acts and lives. A pig with a gold ring in its nose would do the same by rooting in the mud."

"Oh," he exclaimed, "I'm going to preach on that tonight!" I always wondered how he handled that message, but I guess I helped him.

On another occasion we were working our way through the book of James when Ancherai pushed himself away from the table, his eyes filling with tears as was often the case, and exclaimed, "If only all my people could be here listening to your teaching!"

Humbled I replied, "Ancherai, you know that's not possible. That's why *you* must take what *you've* learned and preach it to them." After a week of one-on-one Bible sessions, Ancherai would lift his hand to his chin and say, "*Sahib*, I'm filled up to here. I must leave again on another preaching trip."

In December 1963, Gene Gurganus and I made a survey trip to the Sangu River area with Ancherai. Again our destination was Duniram, that remote Christian village deep in the jungle near the Indian border. Our purpose was to meet with Christian leaders to develop plans for the future of the Tipperah work. Ancherai had sent advance notice of our arrival.

The journey started at Dohazari, a small town 30 miles south of Chittagong city at the juncture of the Sangu River and the Arakan Road. In Dohazari we hired a country boat to transport us and our gear upriver. The boat trip, though slow, was relaxing and we thoroughly enjoyed the jungle scenery along the way. I entertained myself playing the harmonica or reading a book. Floating up the river, Gene remarked, "Jay, just think, we're enjoying all this and getting paid for it, too." How true!

Two days and 25 miles later, we arrived at Boli Bazaar, deep in the Chittagong Hill Tracts. A delegation of Tipperahs met us there to guide us the remaining 12 miles to our destination. Those were tortuous miles. We climbed and descended several mountains and waded across numerous small rivers, or so I thought, until they informed me it was the same river. Had we followed the winding river we would have walked several more hours to reach the village. The way the crow flies is faster.

Frequently the Tipperah guide stopped us to pull off small blood-sucking leeches that attached themselves to our necks, arms, or legs.

I thought we would never reach Duniram. Exhausted, I often asked our guide how much further we had to go. Indicating distance with his voice, he would reply, "*Uuuuuuuuuuurowow.*" An hour later I asked again. He replied with a shorter version of the same sound. The nearer we got to the village the shorter that sound became. "*Urowow*" in Tipperah means "over there." Obviously, *uuuuuuuuuuurowow* meant "way, way over there."

The last mountain rose at a sixty-degree angle. Part way up, totally exhausted, I dug in my heels and leaned back to rest. I remember lying against the side of the mountain, praying and telling God that I would really miss Eleanor and the children, but I was ready to die. I understood then how physically exhausted a person can get.

Finally at the summit, Gene and I saw Duniram Village straddling the top of a mountain below us. Our guide sent a yodeling signal across the valley. While taking a breather before making our final descent, we watched the villagers engage themselves in a swarm of activity. Clouds of dust rose in the air as they swept the ground around their houses. Their excited voices pierced the air as they scurried around, preparing for our arrival. Fatigue forgotten, I loved every minute of it.

The descent was even more difficult because my feet pushed forward in my shoes, creating blisters on the tops of my toes. Relief arrived at the foot of the mountain. A welcoming party received us and washed our feet with cool mountain water that flowed from the heights through bamboo conduits.

Foot washing ceremonies over, the Tipperah elders led us up a trail to the entrance of the village where we were halted behind a large blanket blocking the pathway. Suddenly, at a given signal, the jungle vibrated as a multitude of voices began singing an enchanting tune which we faintly recognized as "Far, Far Away, In Heathen Darkness Dwelling," a hymn they had learned from Chala Lushai. As the singing began they lowered the veil allowing us entrance to the village. My spine began to tingle at the sight. Before us, as far as the eye could see, stood two lines of Tipperahs, women on the left, men on the right, waiting eagerly to shake our hands. What an emotion-packed moment! Those were memorable days as we preached, sang hymns, shared stories, and planned together for the future of the Tipperah work.

One evening after a curry supper the Tipperahs began to pepper us with questions. One curious fellow wanted to know where I lived, to which I replied, "On the other side of the earth. It's evening here in Bangladesh, but it's morning in America where my father and mother live."

Intrigued, yet puzzled by my answer, he asked, "How can that be?"

Picking up a round stone and holding it close to a flickering light, I explained, "The world is round like this stone. This is where we are tonight. Over on that side is where my father and mother live."

He pursued by asking, "How do you know the earth is round?"

"Well," I asked, "is the moon round or flat?"

"Round," he replied, "all you have to do is look."

While he was digesting that thought I zeroed in again, "What about the sun, is it round or flat?" This time he didn't answer, only smiled. He had gotten the point.

Tribal people are gracious hosts. Visitors, especially ones like us, were rare indeed, perhaps arriving only once or twice in a lifetime. They went out of their way to prepare special meals and make us comfortable. Preparing a meal usually meant slaughtering a village pig. We learned later that they only serve pork at weddings or to important guests.

Unfortunately for us, the pig routine happened in every village and we soon tired of pork. The sound of a squealing pig being sacrificed for our benefit quickly lost its appeal. Those docile creatures wandered the village, bellies dragging in the dust, gobbling up garbage and human excrement. Though we often made subtle hints, Gene and I were unsuccessful in convincing our hosts that a scrawny chicken would be just fine.

Then I thought of an idea for a change of menu. After reaching one village and settling for the night, I suggested they serve us venison instead of pork. Excited with that idea, two village hunters borrowed my faithful shotgun and disappeared into the jungle.

A short time later we heard a distant gunshot. *Aha*, I thought, *venison tonight.* I could almost taste it. The hunters soon returned, proudly shouldering a huge Hanuman monkey securely lashed to a bamboo pole, its long tail dragging on the ground.

"Where's the deer?" I asked.

"Well, *Sahib*," they replied, "we saw this monkey first, so we thought we should get meat just in case we didn't see a deer."

I gave them more ammunition and sent them out again. This time they returned with a small deer which they skinned and prepared for cooking. We were pleased to know that we would have venison, not pork, for supper. As we sat eating by the light of a flickering kerosene lamp, however, I detected different textures in the meat. Only then did Gene and I learn that the monkey and deer were cooked in the same pot.

Meetings with the Christian leaders at Duniram village gave us direction for the future of the tribal work. Gene and I came away with three proposals which our Field Council later accepted:

1. That we hold an annual Bible conference at Hebron.
2. That we, at the outset, provide support for the national evangelists.
3. That we provide Bible training for the pastors and evangelists, and literacy training for their children.

On that trip I realized how much Ancherai meant to me. He was more than a brother; he was my teacher. I learned more from him than he could ever know. God gifted him with the ability to draw spiritual applications from his jungle world—stories that illustrated the Word he preached—which resulted in scores of people accepting the Savior. I was so impressed with this humble man of God that I called him "the apostle Paul of the Tipperah people."

One day, after returning from one of his preaching trips, Ancherai told me how he had won an old man to Christ. Ancherai had trekked through mountain trails most of the day. His feet were sore and he was thirsty. Just ahead was a Marma village. He stopped for a drink of water and a rest before proceeding. Marma villages usually consist of 10 to 20 thatched bamboo houses perched on a hill. The houses are always built on stilts with room underneath for the women's weaving looms, firewood, and shelter for the cows, pigs, and chickens. The ground-level inhabitants quickly gobble up scraps of food that fall through the bamboo floors.

As Ancherai approached the village he called out, "Hello! Anybody here?"

Receiving no answer, he walked on and called again. This time an elderly Marma tribesman peered out of a doorway and motioned for Ancherai to enter. Ancherai climbed the notched log and greeted the old man, who was wearing a sarong called a *lungie*. They sat down together on the verandah floor.

"Where is everybody?" the evangelist asked.

"Working in the rice fields," the old man replied. "They'll be back at sundown. They left me here to guard the village."

Marma people farm the mountainsides, as do the other tribes. Finding a lush, jungle-covered mountain, they slash the undergrowth with razor-sharp machetes, let it dry for several weeks, then burn it. The ashes become the fertilizer needed for the rice seed, which is later planted over the burned area. When warm monsoon rains fall, the crops spring to life.

Ancherai, hot and sweaty from walking in the midday sun, told the old man, "I'm very thirsty. Could you give me a drink of water?"

The host disappeared to get a gourd filled with cool water. Meanwhile Ancherai, glancing around the simple hut, saw a brass statue of Buddha perched on an idol shelf above the door. His keen eyes also noted the fresh-cut flowers that recently had been offered to the idol. When the old man returned with the water, he squatted in front of Ancherai.

"*Baba* (a respectful word, meaning father)," Ancherai said as he took the water from the old man, "is that your god up there?"

The wrinkled old man glanced up at the idol and nodded.

Ancherai pointed to the statue. "I see that your god has a mouth. Does he talk with you?"

The tribesman's faded eyes glanced at the idol. He shook his head. "He doesn't talk."

"He has eyes," Ancherai continued. "Can he wink them? Can he really see you?"

A deliberate shake of the head was the only response.

"Well," Ancherai proceeded, "if he can't talk and can't see, then surely he must be able to hear you. Has he ever smiled when you talked with him?"

By this time the old man was visibly irritated. "Of course not," he shot back.

"Who made your god?" Ancherai pursued.

"The silversmith over in Lama Bazar."

Ancherai zeroed in. "*Baba*, isn't the maker of an object greater than the object itself? Why then don't you worship the silversmith?"

As the old gentleman reflected on this amazing proposition, Ancherai continued, "I know the silversmith in Lama Bazar. One day he cheated my wife on some bracelets he made for her. That man is a sinner. He's cheated many people. Yet you are telling me he made your god?"

The old man hung his head as the truth began to penetrate his heart. Ancherai then lifted his Bible from a cloth shoulder bag, opened it, and told the man about his living Savior, the Lord Jesus

Christ. "Jesus can hear, speak, see, and help. He isn't a dead, useless idol. He's alive in heaven and wants you to trust in Him."

Before leaving the village that day, Ancherai heard the old Marma trust Jesus for salvation.

Ancherai was a man who truly "looked for the city which has foundations, whose builder and maker is God" (Hebrews 11:10). He spoke often of heaven. Perhaps the heartaches and hardships he suffered on earth made him long for the presence of God. I'll always remember the day when the late Dr. R. T. Ketcham spoke to the tribal Bible school students. He spoke on Psalm 23 while I translated his message for the students. After the meeting, I introduced Ancherai to Dr. Ketcham, explaining that he was already 80 years old. Grinning from ear to ear, and raising his hand close to my face, Ancherai formed a small crack between his thumb and forefinger. "Just think," he exclaimed in Tipperah, "he's only this far away from seeing Jesus. Isn't that wonderful?"

Though Ancherai had often talked and dreamed about heaven, I was shocked when the sad news of his death reached me. During my years of working with him he had often complained of severe pains in his abdomen. Time and again I sent him for medical tests but no significant problem could be detected.

Eleanor and I were visiting our children in Murree, Pakistan when Ancherai was admitted to the hospital with severe pain. Not responding to treatment, he died on August 4, 1978 and entered the presence of the Lord he loved and served.

Ancherai's son, Daniel, one of his eight children, was at his father's bedside when he died. Daniel told me this story: "My father was in much pain and refused to eat the food we had prepared for him. Suddenly, he sat up in bed and a broad smile filled his face. 'Look!' he exclaimed, 'See the angels descending? They're coming to take me to Jesus!' After blurting out those words, and still pointing towards heaven, he fell back dead on his pillow."

In my report to mission headquarters I wrote, "The home-going of Ancherai Tipperah is another reminder of the passage of time.

His death ended a special era in the ministry of the ABWE in Bangladesh. The world has to be a darker, sadder place without him. Ancherai was my friend and disciple for 18 years. He was also my teacher. We shared many wonderful years together. But I alone cannot claim a special relationship with this dear brother because he endeared himself to all of our missionaries. His love reached out to all who knew him."

A marvelous chapter in the history of our tribal ministry ended on that August day. Only eternity will reveal the spiritual fruit that Ancherai, apostle to the Tipperahs, bore during his lifetime.

THE PRIMITIVE MURUNGS

*"And he (Jesus) said unto them, Go ye into
all the world, and preach the gospel to every
creature"*
Mark 16:15

Of all the tribal groups living in the Chittagong Hill Tracts, the semi-nomadic Murungs are the most primitive. They live in remote, almost inaccessible areas and have limited contact with the outside world. The men dress in G-strings; the women wear topless mini-skirts. Their nakedness may be one of the reasons for their shyness. But we have found the Murungs to be a lovable, beautiful people—a people encompassed by God's love and for whom Christ died. They, too, must hear the gospel message.

The first Murungs whom Eleanor and I came to know were Langrau and Edoi, who worked for the mission after we moved to Hebron. Langrau, a tall, muscular man, kept our storage barrels filled with Matamahari River water because at that time we had no well at Hebron. After several months on the job, Langrau left one weekend for his village and never returned. No doubt he preferred jungle life to the "civilized" life of Hebron. We really missed him.

Then there was Edoi, a short, balding man of quiet disposition. I hired him to help Eleanor with the children and the household chores. Our Phillip was a baby then, and Edoi loved toting him around. When he was working in the house Edoi preferred hopping in and out of our large windows rather than using the doors. He often called me to shoot bats or rats for his curry, which he was always eager to share with us. Edoi, too, decided to leave one day. We learned later that he had gotten married. We never saw either of these men again but prayed that our witness to them might one day bear fruit.

Some years later we hired another Murung man and wife, Ahdee and Mru, to work as *malis* (gardeners). They were excellent gardeners, fun to have around, and entertaining with their unusual sense of humor. One morning as we were eating breakfast, Mru popped in the doorway proudly displaying a wriggling rat which she was squeezing firmly by its neck. Noticing blood on her hand I asked her how she had caught it.

"With my hand, can't you see?" she replied.

She informed us that a family of rats had burrowed holes in the garden and were eating the vegetables at night. That had to stop. She squatted patiently behind one of the rat holes with her hand poised for action. When the rat poked out its head, she quickly grabbed it by the neck. In its struggle to get free, the rat nipped her finger.

As she stood beside our table with the rat dangling from her hand, she tapped it on the belly with her machete and exclaimed, "Look, it's a male." As if we wanted to know!

Another time her husband, Ahdee, caught a three-foot monitor lizard, a Murung delicacy. He had pulled its long, tapered tail up over its back and tied it to the neck with a piece of thin wire. He then bound its feet to make sure it didn't escape. When he came to show us his prize, Adhee was carrying it like a woman carries a purse.

By late afternoon, the reptile had managed somehow to gnaw through the wire and made a determined effort to reach jungle cover. Mru, however, spotted it trying to escape and dispatched it with one quick swipe of her machete. They enjoyed the meat and we inherited the skin.

Murung men are easily distinguished from other tribal men. They keep their shoulder-length hair rolled into a bun and skewered neatly on the left side of the head. They sometimes wear turbans and almost always keep a colorful comb parked in the bun. Freshly cut flowers, poked through the holes of their pierced ears, are common. Murung men, especially the marriageable young ones, paint their bodies with a red dye which they think makes them attractive to the opposite sex. Their teeth, blackened with wood ash, really set them apart from other ethnic groups.

One day a great commotion at the Hebron clinic drew our attention. A large group of colorful Murungs arrived bearing an unconscious young man who had been mauled by a wild boar. Mary Lou called for help and together we carefully cleaned and dressed his gaping wounds. Though he had lost plenty of blood because of his injuries, he most likely fainted from fright. Wild pigs, especially angry boars, are ferocious when they attack. When our patient revived and saw strange white faces hovering over him, he was struck with yet another pang of fear.

The "Pig Murung," as he was known to the missionaries, later recalled his frightening experience. He and his wife had been cutting bamboo deep in a jungle forest when their hunting dog, roaming the area, jumped a sleeping boar. Startled, the tusker charged the dog which ran to its master. At that point the boar stopped chasing the elusive dog and attacked its owner.

By the time his screaming wife drove off the pig, her husband lay on the ground writhing in pain. The boar, with its razor-sharp tusks, had punctured his abdomen and one of his hands. It had also bitten him in several places, tearing away flesh as if biting from an apple. Splattered with blood, matted hair drooping to his shoulders, and wearing only a G-string, our patient certainly looked like a wild man.

The Pig Murung stayed with us for almost a month while we treated his wounds. As his condition improved, he followed me around, observing me at work. He was as curious about me as I was about him. I was especially fascinated with his hunting skills. He cleverly snared squirrels and rats with his own unique inventions. I watched as he shot birds with a bamboo dart gun and trapped others by smearing sticky glue on tree limbs, enticing them to land with a few grains of rice. His ingenuity and intelligence greatly impressed me and helped me understand how the Murung people survived in their jungle world.

Fully recovered, the Pig Murung bade us good-bye and returned to his home many miles east of Hebron near the Burma border. A week later, a long canoe loaded with Murungs docked at Hebron. The men struggled up the river bank carrying a huge domestic pig secured in a bamboo cage. "It's for you missionaries, *Sahib*," the Pig Murung said. We knew it was a thanksgiving offering for the treatment we had given and the hospitality we had shown.

"How about slaughtering it now?" I suggested. "Then we can celebrate together." My idea appealed to them. That evening we sat in a circle on bamboo mats, eating pork curry served on green banana leaves.

ABWE's first contact with the Murung tribe occurred in March 1957 when Rev. and Mrs. Barnard and Paul Miller made a survey of the southern Chittagong Hill Tracts. They traveled by an ancient DC-3 plane to the seaside town of Cox's Bazar, then by Jeep 10 miles east to the village of Ramu. From there they traveled east up the Baghkhali River, first by canoe, until the intermittent river became too shallow to navigate, then by foot.

Paul recorded in his journal, "At 3:00 p.m. we reached our first Murung village. After a time of curious stares at each other, the headman brought rice and eggs. The latter were duly passed from one person to another and shaken to test for soundness, then given to us. I found one young fellow who knew about as much Bengali as I did, so I proceeded to get Murung words and write them phonetically. The atmosphere became increasingly friendly. After our meal we read the Bible and prayed. The Barnards were tired and so settled down under their mosquito nets for the night.

The Walshes with Tom and Olline McDonald

Jay and Ancherai teaching Bible stories.

Just call me "Daniel"

Jay helped tribals to purchase shotguns.

Murung tribesman with his
evening meal

AGAINST ALL ODDS

A VENTURE OF FAITH
WITH THE HILL TRIBES
OF BANGLADESH

View of Duniram Tipperah Village

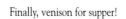

Finally, venison for supper!

Left: Wild boar

Men from the Murung tribe

The evacuation group of 34 safe in Bangkok, Thailand

Jay meets Sheik Mujibur Rahman, the father of the new nation of Bangladesh.

Above:
Debapriya Roy, who translated the Chakma New Testament

Left:
Mr. M.L.S. Colney, the Lushai "Senator" from Mizoram

Jay and Vicki Shaw finalizing the Tipperah New Testament.

Pastor Gunijon Tipperah and missionary George Collins

Tipperah young people using their new hymn book for the first time.

Evangelist Robichandro and Pastor Gunijon Tipperah with the Walshes on dedication day

I sat on a log by the fire with four of the men. I explained to one of them that we had read from God's book in English, and that we also have it in Bengali. He gazed at the fire wistfully and said, 'Yes, it's in English and in Bengali, but not in Murung.' Oh, how I wished that it were! That's a job yet to be done."

Paul Miller would never do that job. Just two months later, and only two weeks after moving to Hebron to begin his translation work, he died of polio on May 3, 1959. His grave marker in the Christian cemetery in Chittagong says it all:

REV. PAUL MORRIS MILLER

JAN. 4, 1917–MAY 3, 1959

BIRTH PLACE–ST. LOUIS, MO, USA

"TO ME TO LIVE IS CHRIST

AND TO DIE IS GAIN"

Not until Rev. Harry Goehring and I traveled into the Chittagong Hill Tracts in 1963 did we really began to understand the Murung people and their religious practices. Harry and his wife, Nancy, had come to Bangladesh to work with the tribes. I now had the special opportunity and privilege of introducing Harry to the people of the hills.

That morning, as we drifted down the Sangu River, we noticed several Murungs skinning an animal near the water's edge. Curious, we docked the canoe and walked over to observe the activity. The worshipers had built a bamboo altar on which they had sacrificed a goat. Blood still dripped from the altar, staining the sand below. The skull of the goat remained in place on the altar. Men were busy cutting up the meat, apparently for a feast.

Harry later wrote about that experience, "How often I had heard of these primitive people living far back in the inaccessible jungle hills. Four sullen faced men, their reddish-brown bodies clothed only in loincloths, watched curiously as Jay and I drifted slowly past in our country boat.

"Their curiosity was no greater than our own. How interesting they were with their long, black hair tied in a knot on one side of their heads. Beautiful jungle orchids decorated the lobes of their ears and red paint was smeared on their cheeks. These were the primitive Murungs."

An interpreter helped us understand why they had sacrificed the goat. A spokesman for the group explained, "*Shoitan* (Satan) is oppressing our village. Many of our people are sick and some have died. We want to make him happy so he'll leave and stop causing us trouble."

It was clear to Harry and me that they were not Satan worshipers but Satan appeasers. They feared that unseen evil spirit and believed a blood sacrifice would expedite his departure from their village. We left the scene with heavy hearts. Here was a tribe whose language was yet to be learned, a tribe that needed to hear of the cleansing blood of Christ.

Trekking in the Matamahari Valley later that same year, evangelist Ancherai Tipperah and I arrived at a large Murung village whose headman, Meypong, had just sacrificed a cow. The helpless animal had been securely tethered to a tree in the center of the village. When an orchestra of bamboo musical pipes began to drone, and women began to dance, the men of the village, intoxicated by rice whiskey, circled the doomed cow, piercing it with spears until it died from loss of blood. Meypong explained that the cow sacrifice was an annual religious ceremony in Murung villages.

The cow sacrifice ritual, we learned, started from a legend passed down by the Murung forefathers. According to legend, *Torai*, the Great Spirit, gave a written language and moral code to all people, but somehow the Murungs had been left out. In desperation, their forefathers sent a cow to the Great Spirit to ask for help. He responded by writing a code of rules for them on banana leaves. To their great horror and eternal loss, the cow ate the leaves on its return journey. Proof for this, they say, is on the inside of the cow's stomach which is very rough, damaged by eating the sacred writings. The annual cow sacrifice is the Murungs' way of getting even.

Meypong Murung was one of the first of his tribe to become a Christian. He lived in the mountain range separating the Sangu and Matamahari valleys. Ancherai, on return trips to that village, preached to Meypong about the sacrifice of Christ on Calvary. Meypong received Christ as His Savior and began to travel with Ancherai on preaching tours. He also began to attend our annual short-term Bible schools held at Hebron where he grew in his Christian life.

The Goehrings, with their three small children, Harold, Faith and Joy, moved to Hebron in 1964 while Eleanor and I furloughed in the USA. The Goehrings learned more about the various tribal groups, including the Murungs. In a report dated March 24, 1965, Harry wrote:

"During the past few months we have witnessed a general movement among the Murungs. On many occasions, Murungs from different villages have come to our door stating that they wanted to become Christians. Through our helpers we have inquired as to the reason. Occasionally, it was obvious that there was a physical motive involved, but the majority of the individuals stated that they had heard of Christianity through another Murung and wanted to receive it. We feel that much of this openness is a result of the work of Meypong Murung. He has shown real interest in the gospel, not just for himself but for all the hill people. He has brought people to us desiring to become Christians and has begged us to preach in other villages."

Harry went on to write, "While this apparent openness in the Murung tribe causes us to rejoice, it brings with it a great burden and responsibility to do all we can to reach that tribe with the Gospel. All we can do at present is to accompany evangelist Ancherai on weekly trips into various villages when he is available to go. However, the only real answer is for God to separate unto this tribe another Ancherai from among their own people."

Meypong later named one of his sons "Gerring" after Harry, who had come to Bangladesh specifically to take up the tribal translation ministry that Paul Miller had left undone. For reasons known only to an omniscient and loving God, two-and-one-half months after penning the above report, Harry died. A gravestone in the compound of the Memorial Christian Hospital tells the story:

HARRY DALE GOEHRING
16 APRIL, 1933–16 JUNE, 1965
"WITH CHRIST" MARK 8:34,35

In 1966 I hired Robichandro (Robi) to be my Tipperah language teacher. He moved his family from Duniram Village in the Sangu to Chimpru Village, much nearer to the hospital where we were living at that time. He spent weekdays teaching me Tipperah and weekends with his family. Eventually, because of the inconvenience of travel and the expense involved, Robi moved his family to the hospital compound where he and I, along with evangelist Ancherai, completed a Tipperah dictionary and grammar.

A major breakthrough in reaching the Murungs for Christ came unexpectedly through Robi in the fall of 1973. Besides working with me in Tipperah, Robichandro also took on the responsibility of hospital evangelist for tribal patients, some of whom were Murungs. About that same time the mission had purchased an additional 18 acres of jungle for expanding the hospital. This land had to be cleared and tribal people, who farmed the jungle-covered mountains by the slash and burn method, were especially qualified for the job. At my request Robi spread the word in the hills that we were going to hire jungle cutters in a "food for work" program.

Robi and I had expected Tipperah people to respond to our announcement. Instead, a whole village of Murung tribesmen appeared. Our food for work program appealed to them because they were facing famine in their area. They responded because they were hungry.

The Murung men began their work in earnest, with the women and children helping. What a sight that was! Those simple people, clad in G-strings and mini-skirts, began swinging their sharp machetes, slashing the thorny jungle to the ground.

After work the men and boys disappeared into the nearby forest to hunt for their evening meal—a tree lizard, a stray dog, or simply jungle vegetation to be eaten with boiled rice. After their meal they squatted around open fires, jabbering and warming themselves.

Recognizing an opportune time to witness for Christ, Robi and I captured their attention with Bible story flash cards. He was an expert in using those tools to preach God's Word to an illiterate audience. By the end of the second week Robi, all smiles, said to me, "*Sahib*, four of the Murung leaders have trusted Christ. Would you allow them to give their testimonies in church next Sunday?" Just like that.

My first reaction was to shout, "Hallelujah!" Then I pressed Robi for more details. Were the Murungs really saved? Are you sure they understand the gospel? Are they becoming Christians to keep their employment? (This happens so often that we tend to become extremely cautious about professions of faith.)

Robi convinced me that they indeed had been born again. The following Sunday morning, tears of joy filled many eyes as we listened to those Murung believers boldly tell of their new-found faith in Christ. We had witnessed a great opening in the Murung tribe. After the jungle clearing project was finished and they returned to their homes, Robi continued to teach them, making periodic preaching trips to their village.

One day Robi appeared at the door with a group of Murung men. When I greeted them they handed me a gift, a big rooster. That, too, was usually a tip-off that they wanted some kind of help, probably a loan.

"Not so," explained Robi. "They have a special request for

you." He pulled a piece of paper from a bamboo tube and handed it to me. The note had obviously been composed by a professional Bengali letter writer because this tribe was totally illiterate. "It's from the Murungs," he said. "They have built a 'Jesus House' in their village and they want you to dedicate it." The gift of a rooster was a petition to convince me to attend the dedication.

Robi was insistent, and my sense of being part of history in the making overruled other considerations. We began the 14-mile trek early, walking steadily throughout the long, hot day. Finally, as the sun was sinking below the mountains behind us, we arrived at their village. After entering the compound, the proud Murung believers led me straight to their "Jesus House." The shiny new bamboo church sat in the center of the village, decorated with clusters of wild flowers, including multicolored orchids. I gave a brief message in Chittagonian, the *lingua franca* of the Hill Tracts, and uttered a dedicatory prayer. Robi, never one for the limelight, stood in the background taking it all in like a proud father.

Robichandro continues to play a major role in Murung evangelism. At Hebron in 1981, he baptized a young man named Chongtai Murung who now serves as one of the leaders of the Murung church. In his leadership role, Chongtai, who plays a handmade guitar, has been especially influential in teaching hymns to his people.

One day, at a Murung Bible seminar, Chongtai and his wife led a singing class with the aid of his guitar. Curiosity getting the best of me, I asked, "Chongtai, who taught you to play the guitar? And where did you learn those hymns?"

"From Chingtai Murung, the song master," he replied. "He's that old man over there." This was a revelation to me. Sometime in Murung history someone had taught music to Chingtai. I interviewed the Murung song master. To my delight, he also told me of the Lushai connection. Chingtai came from the northern Sangu River area and had lived with the Bawm people, a tribe ethnically related to the Murungs. The Bawms had been converted to Christ by Lushai evangelists in the early part of the 20th century. Chingtai spoke of two Murung Christians, Chunglok and Laikoi, who had gone to Aizawl, Mizoram, for training. They learned to read and write Roman script. Upon returning to the Sangu area, these men composed a Murung hymnbook of 75 songs which they had learned from the Lushais. He also told me that Chunglok was now very old but still living in Chimbok Village near the Indian border.

The Murung tribe, numbering over 20,000 in Bangladesh, with thousands more living in Myanmar (Burma), is still largely an unreached tribe. In God's timing, this will change. The real story about the primitive Murungs is yet to unfold.

CHAPTER 16

SOUNDS TO SENTENCES

*"But the word of the Lord endureth forever. And
this is the word which by the gospel is preached
unto you."*

1 Peter 1:25

Missionaries engaged in tribal evangelism any place in the
world sooner or later find themselves involved in translation.
After establishing contact with a target population, they must
learn that language and reduce it to writing. At first the Tipperah
language struck me as a babble of strange sounds but later, when I
phonetically transcribed them to paper, they began to make sense.
After months of effort I began to speak the language haltingly. In
time, I became more fluent and was able to communicate, not
only about trivial matters, but of deeper spiritual realities. When
that was possible, it became my passion to translate the Bible for
the people I loved. Translation work, I learned, is an enormous
task requiring years of patient and diligent work.

On the wall of our Bible translation room in Chittagong hangs
a plaque quoting missionary to China Robert Morrison, who elo-
quently describes translation work like this:

"The duty of a translator of any book is twofold. First, to comprehend
accurately the sense, and to feel the spirit of the original work; and secondly, to express in his version faithfully, perspicuously, and idiomatically
(and, if he can attain it, elegantly), the sense and spirit of the original."

With that mindset, Joyce Ann Wingo moved to Hebron in 1959 to begin learning the Tipperah language. The field minutes of June 5, 1959, state, "Miss Wingo requests field council permission to move to Hebron at this time to begin work on the Tipperah language, which is as yet unwritten."

That motion carried with it the stipulation that "she be set apart specifically to work on reducing the Tipperah language to writing, which is to preclude any other station responsibilities. The field council feels that such work is vitally essential since there is widespread interest among the Tipperahs towards the Gospel." In November of that year Joyce Ann and nurse Mary Lou Brownell moved to Hebron. Eleanor and I joined them six months later.

Before leaving for furlough in March 1962, Joyce Ann successfully translated the Gospel of John in Tipperah using the Roman script. Later, the thought-provoking question arose in the Bible translation committee as to whether or not it would be more advantageous to translate the Bible using the Bengali script. After researching that question, the Bible translation committee and the Tipperah leaders agreed that, since many of their young people were already learning to read and write Bengali in government schools, the Bengali script should be used in translating the Bible into Tipperah. After prayerful consideration, the mission agreed with that concept as the *modus operandi* for the future translation of tribal languages.

Other factors favored this change. As a minority group in Bangladesh, the Tipperahs would have a closer tie with the rest of the country if the Bengali alphabet were used. More importantly, using the Bengali script would eliminate the laborious and time-consuming task of having to teach the English alphabet to the Tipperahs.

Joyce Ann had turned over to the Hebron missionaries a notebook of Tipperah words and a bundle of John's Gospels which she had mimeographed. That industrious work provided the basis for the translation we expected her to continue when she returned. It was our great loss when we learned that she would be getting married and not returning to Bangladesh. The Tipperah youth with whom she worked were also disappointed and greatly missed her. In a matter of months she had endeared herself to a tribe who, even today, speak sentimentally of her visits to their villages.

After the death of Harry Goehring in 1965, I assumed responsibility for the Tipperah translation project. At first I felt at a disadvantage because I had not been trained in translation techniques as Joyce Ann had. However, like her, I had a deep love for the Tipperah people and a compelling desire to learn their language. That worked to my advantage. With evangelist Ancherai as my assistant, I began translating miscellaneous Bible verses, key promises of God that I had learned in my youth. This gave me a feel for the enormous task that lay ahead. Slowly, over a period of weeks, we found that we could capture all the Tipperah sounds by using the Bengali alphabet. That made our work much easier and faster, confirming our earlier decision.

I continued to compile new vocabulary words which I added to Joyce Ann's list. As the list grew in size, I couldn't help but be amazed at the depth of the Tipperah language. No matter what subject we discussed—excluding, perhaps, modern scientific jargon—they had a word or a description for it. During the politically unstable year of 1970, Ancherai, Robichandro and I, with the assistance of my colleague Lynn Silvernale, the coordinator of the Bengali Bible translation project, completed a 2,500-word dictionary and simple grammar. We spent long hours on that project which provided the basis for future translation work.

Between 1965 and 1978, when evangelist Ancherai died, we had many interruptions in the translation work, including the 1971 Bangladesh War of Independence. During that period, however, Ancherai and I retranslated the Gospel of John, benefiting greatly from Joyce Ann's original work. We also completed first-draft translations of James and the Gospel of Mark, plus several of the Psalms. When the tribal churches began to formally organize, we translated important documents for them including a doctrinal statement, a church covenant, and a sample constitution and by-laws.

In November 1977, Ancherai and I and Debapriya Roy, a new believer from the large Chakma tribe, attended a translators' workshop in Dhaka. After that valuable learning experience, Ancherai and I translated the New Reader Series of Bible stories (five booklets) for newly literate people. For future evangelism, we also translated several tracts with titles such as *Creation To Christ, Fear of Evil Spirits, Why Jesus Had To Die, Which Path?, How The Christian Lives*, and *Life After Death*. That special training in Dhaka also proved to be the motivating factor for Debapriya, a para-plegic, to take up the difficult task of translating the New Testament into the Chakma language.

Debapriya Roy, a member of the Chakma royal family and first cousin of the present Chakma king, was permanently disabled in a motorcycle accident in Rangamati, capital of the Chittagong Hill Tracts. He became a Christian in our hospital and was later baptized, wheelchair and all! During the months of his treatment and rehabilitation, he completed several Moody Bible Institute correspondence courses.

Eager to reach his own people for Christ, Debapriya sought advice as to how that vision might be fulfilled, even though he would be confined to a wheelchair for the rest of his life. The Chakmas, numbering more than a quarter million people, repre-sent the largest tribe in Bangladesh. Before Debapriya returned to Rangamati, Dr. Vic Olsen and I spent days helping him develop a plan for evangelizing his tribe, suggesting the important role he could play. A major aspect of that plan included his writing gospel tracts and translating the New Testament.

It took time for Debapriya to adjust to the fact that he would spend the rest of his life in a wheelchair. Eventually, however, he accepted his situation as being God's plan for giving him quality time for the translation project and the evangelization of his people. Under mission supervision, and with the special assistance of Vicki Shaw, Debapriya completed the New Testament, making the Word of God available for the first time to the largest tribe in the Chittagong Hill Tracts.

In time, the Sangu Tipperah Christians began pressing us to translate a hymnbook. They loved to sing and had already committed to memory many hymns that had been handed down by the Lushai evangelists. But they had also composed new hymns and choruses based on memory verses they had learned at our Bible conferences at Hebron. These also needed to be published.

Before Ancherai's death in 1978, I hired an educated young man named Rambadu, a Sangu area Tipperah, to help me with translation. He was especially eager to compile a hymnbook first and I agreed. The first 500-copy edition of that book, containing 81 hymns and choruses, came off our own ABC press in Chittagong in September 1978. A decade later we printed 2,000 copies of a larger, revised edition containing 122 songs.

With Ancherai gone, I recognized in Rambadu the talent necessary to proceed with the translation of the New Testament. He was an independent thinker, and had the intelligence and tenacity needed for such a painstaking job. The Lord sent to us Vicki Shaw, a talented and motivated missionary translator whom God had called to work in Bangladesh. With her expertise and technical help, we finalized the gospel of Mark which rolled off the press on May 22, 1990.

Our special team of translators and checkers have since completed the translation of the entire Tipperah New Testament. That project took thousands of dedicated work hours over a period of 30 years, but the Tipperah people now have the eternal Word of God in their own beautiful language.

And what about the Murung Scriptures? When Paul Miller made his first contact with a Murung village in 1959, one of the men said to him in reference to the Bible, "Yes, it's in English and in Bengali, but not in Murung." That statement gave Paul a vision and burden for the Murung tribe. Sadly, that burden died with him. Several years later, history repeated itself as Harry Goehring also died. Today, however, Harry's son, Harold, has answered the call of God to work with the Murung tribe. He is studying their language with plans to see that the Word of God is accurately translated for them.

But there is more to this wonderful story. On June 20, 1995, Eleanor and I drove our son Phillip, his talented wife Becky, and their infant daughter Sophia, to the Kent County International Airport in Grand Rapids, Michigan to see them off for Bangladesh. Phillip was born 35 years earlier, only two months after we arrived in that land. As we proudly watched them board their flight, we knew they were planning to work with the Rakhine tribe, an ethnic group living in Bangladesh but whose roots and major population are in the Arakan District of Myanmar. A talented linguist, Phillip will be translating God's Word for yet another tribe for whom Christ died.

CHAPTER 17

INTERRUPTED BY REVOLUTION

*"I would seek unto God, and unto God would
I commit my cause, Who doeth great things
and unsearchable, marvelous things without
number."*
Job 5:8–9

March 1971 marked the beginning of Eleanor's and my second decade in Bangladesh. That was also the year when West Pakistan's control over East Pakistan ended. Until then, Pakistan was composed of two wings located on opposite sides of India.

In December 1970, one of East Pakistan's most devastating cyclones thrashed in fury through the islands and coastal areas, killing more than 500,000 people in one night. Bengali political leaders, with some justification, were outraged with the central government, located in West Pakistan, which had not made determined or sufficient efforts to provide relief and rehabilitation for the suffering people of the eastern wing. From their perspective, however, the central government had good reasons for being calloused. At that very time Bengali politicians were actively making plans to secede from the union. East Pakistan, fed up with being controlled by West Pakistan for more than 23 years, wanted independence. A nation called Bangladesh, meaning the land of people whose language is Bengali, was their dream.

The political general election which followed that catastrophic cyclone of 1970 made it abundantly clear that the people of East Pakistan had made their decision. Nothing could divert them now from the path of independence. In March 1971, three months after the cyclone, Bengali patriot Sheik Mujibur Rahman's Awami League Party won the national elections. Embarrassed and reluctant to hand over power to Sheik Mujib, the Pakistani ruling leaders became involved in political stalling tactics. Impatient and angry, the Bengali population rebelled and rose up to declare the birth of a new nation. A civil war erupted!

In one final, determined effort to subdue the rebellion and save the union, Pakistani generals arrested Sheik Mujib and secretly flew him across India to West Pakistan where he was incarcerated. They then deployed their troops who crisscrossed East Pakistan on a killing, raping, and burning campaign. The genocide that followed within the next nine months left over three million Bengalis dead. That suppressive campaign also became a threat to the safety of all missionaries, including those of us with ABWE.

Prior to the Bangladeshi declaration of independence on March 26, 1971, and sensing that major political trouble was brewing in the country, I met with the American consul general regarding the option of evacuating our missionaries to safety through Burma, if that seemed prudent. He agreed with the idea and promised to relay a message of that possibility to the American Embassy in Rangoon.

As April wore on, rumors of unspeakable atrocities continued to reach our ears. In preparation for the worst scenario, we organized an evacuation committee who identified three possible routes for escape. One was the canal route through the mangrove swamps to the Bay of Bengal, then down the coastline to Burma. We would keep a sampan ready for that eventuality. Another plan called for taking refuge in the Chittagong Hill Tracts, which involved hiking eastward on jungle trails. There we could wait out the civil war as guests of the tribal Christians. The third plan, and the one we eventually used, was to travel by vehicle 85 miles south to Teknaf, the southernmost town in Bangladesh. There, we would cross the three-mile-wide Naf River to Maungdao, Burma. We all came to the decision, however, that no evacuation would take place unless the Lord gave us a specific sign to do so.

I had been meeting regularly with tribal leaders to keep them informed about the deteriorating situation in the country and about the possibility of missionary evacuation. I also assured them that I, personally, had no plans to leave Bangladesh unless God made that decision abundantly clear. The tribal leaders, while fearful of what could happen, knew that they were reasonably safe in their jungle havens.

At 11:00 p.m. on April 20, Director of Nursing, Becky Davey, unable to sleep, tuned her shortwave radio to the Voice of America (VOA). She could hardly believe her ears!

"Now a special announcement for the Americans working at the Malumghat hospital. The U.S. government strongly advises all but essential personnel to proceed immediately by motor vehicle to Burma. The Chittagong exit is no longer available. Repeat . . . ."

Up until then, evacuation through the seaport city of Chittagong had been possible. Some of our missionaries, those whose furloughs were due, had left East Pakistan before the VOA announcement aired.

Becky's catching that announcement was the first miracle of a series that would follow. She was the *only* person who heard it. We learned later that VOA repeated the same message the following morning at 7:00 a.m. By then we had departed for Burma.

Thirty-seven ABWE missionaries, including women and children, were still in the country when the VOA announcement was made. Rev. Reid Minich opted to remain in Chittagong as the only ABWE missionary to minister to the national Christians and to look after our properties there. The other Chittagong missionaries, Jeannie Lockerbie and Lynn Silvernale, had brought nationals to

Malumghat for safety. They all had planned to sit out the scrimmage there. That made 36 ABWE missionaries and children at Malumghat.

At midnight, unable to get further confirmation of the VOA announcement, as field chairman I called the missionaries together for a meeting. We all agreed that the VOA announcement was God's way of getting our attention. In that historic meeting I was elected evacuation leader, replacing Rev. Melvin Beals who had been chosen for the job earlier but had already left for Burma on a family vacation prior to the VOA announcement. Doctors Viggo Olsen and Donn Ketcham would remain behind to care for medical emergencies, and to protect the staff and hospital property. Each of us would begin immediately to pack valuables in barrels, readying them for shipment in the event that we could never return. Each family would be allowed two suitcases for the evacuation trip; singles, one.

On that auspicious night the second "miracle" took place. The government electric supply, which during previous nights had been switched off at 10:00 p.m. to conserve a dwindling fuel supply, stayed on until 4:00 a.m., allowing us time to finish our work.

At 6:00 a.m., April 21, after a two-hour rest and a hurried breakfast, we missionaries loaded three hospital vehicles and drove south to Teknaf, a four-hour journey over narrow, rough roads. In Teknaf, anticipating that we might need Burmese money, I located a shopkeeper who agreed to an exchange. That hunch proved to be providential. Our first expenditure was renting a Burmese fishing sampan which we dubbed "Noah's ark." In that we crossed the Naf River to Maungdao, a sleepy Burmese town known locally as a smuggling center.

During the river crossing, Dr. Joe DeCook's wife, Joyce, accidentally dropped one of her contact lenses which fell to the greasy bottom of the sampan. She couldn't see without it and had no spare. Finding an object that small seemed next to impossible but,

determined to make the effort, we searched and, to our amazement, found it. Miracle number three.

The Burmese authorities in Maungdao received us cordially.
After a passport check and registration, they lodged us for the
night in a government guest house. We all lay sprawled on the
floor in two huge rooms where we slept fitfully until daybreak.

At 10:00 a.m. on April 22, approval came from Rangoon for
Maungdao immigration officials to move us to the southern port
city of Akyab where American embassy officials from Rangoon
would meet us. They loaded us like cattle into two World War II
vintage trucks and drove us under armed guard 16 miles east to the
village of Buthidaung on the Mayu River. There we crowded into
an ancient steel launch for the 80-mile trip.

We arrived late that same night at the estuary of the Mayu
River and the Bay of Bengal. The lighting system on the launch
had failed, leaving us—literally—in the dark. The captain also
failed to locate a feeder canal that would lead us into Akyab town.
To complicate matters, a storm was brewing in the Bay. Our
launch, overloaded with 40 people, including the boatmen and
four immigration officers, kept circling in an attempt to find our
port. Occasionally the launch hit bottom. Fearful of a pending
accident, Joe and I persuaded the authorities to drop anchor for
the night and wait out the storm.

We spent a miserable night as the launch, buffeted by wind and
rain, bobbed up and down like a cork in a bathtub. Several of us,
not finding space under cover, clung to ropes on the open deck. By
early morning the storm played itself out, as the day dawned bright
and beautiful.

The boatman and immigration officers, having determined
they had overshot the entrance to Akyab, told us that we had to
go back upriver a mile or so. When the launch engine refused to
start because of a dead battery, the boatmen simply hoisted the
anchor and let the incoming tide drift us up river.

The tide was working in our favor but the wind wasn't—it kept angling us to the port side. Several of us men, pushing hard with long bamboo poles that had been lashed to the sides of the launch, made a gallant effort to keep the boat in midstream. However, we lost the battle. The wind beached us, while ebb tide left us stranded high and dry on the sand. That's when we all jumped out to stretch while the immigration officials commandeered a small fishing boat and left to get help.

Our gang was hungry, since we had finished the last of the evacuation rations the night before. After the officials departed, I signaled two young boys passing in a canoe and hired them to take me to a bazaar where I could buy food. Eager for *baksheesh* (a tip), they paddled me up a narrow canal to a nearby tribal hamlet. The people, looking much like the Marmas of Bangladesh, appeared dumbfounded to see this foreigner wandering about their village. Obviously, my presence was a first for them. I smiled and greeted people as I ambled by their homes purchasing everything in sight that would be safe to eat, including cookies and bananas. The Burmese currency I had purchased in Teknaf was a godsend. Bazaaring finished, the boys, who spoke the Chittagonian dialect, returned me to the launch. My colleagues were pleased to get the food but the immigration officials, who in the meantime had returned, were irate. Where I had been shopping was an area of Communist insurgency, harboring active anti-government guerrillas!

Eventually, a slick Burmese PT boat arrived in mid-river and took us to the entrance of the large canal we had missed the night before. There we were off-loaded into dinghies and paddled through the canal to the port where American embassy officials were waiting to receive us. As we approached the reception party we were singing the chorus, "With Christ in my vessel I can smile at the storm." Later, on the short flight to Rangoon, I sat beside Colonel Walsh (no relation), Air Force attaché with the

American embassy, who remarked, "I've been involved in many evacuations in my time, but I've never met a group as happy and composed as you people."

As we stood chatting with our reception party, enjoying snacks and cold drinks, the American consul, Mr. Gene Martin, told me that Burmese army officials had requested a short interview with the evacuation leader.

"They want to know what's happening across the border," he explained. "They will limit their questions to 10 minutes."

I agreed to the interview but requested that fellow missionary Mel Beals accompany me as a witness. We had met up with the Beals family at the government guest house in Maungdao.

A military jeep, bristling with rifles, whisked us away to army headquarters where we were introduced to a tough looking colonel. He sat sober-faced at a huge teakwood desk in front of a long table. Mel and I were seated on opposite sides of the table near the colonel, with other Burmese officials seated around us. An interpreter sat between the colonel and me, and a male typist sat at the end of the table facing the colonel. The interrogation was a comedy. The colonel asked a question in Burmese which the interpreter repeated to me in English. I then conferred with Mel, in English, as to how I would reply. The interpreter then relayed my answer in Burmese to the colonel, who repeated it to the typist in Burmese who, in turn, typed it in English!

With this circus going on, the ten minutes stretched quickly into an hour. Upset by the delay, Mr. Martin, who had taken the rest of the missionaries to a guest house for lunch, suddenly barged into the room. He scolded the colonel for exceeding the time agreement, then escorted Mel and me to a waiting vehicle. We joined our colleagues at the Akyab airport, boarding a chartered Union of Burma DC-3 for the short flight to Rangoon.

The American ambassador, Mr. Hummel, along with his political officer, Mr. Fleck, greeted our plane in Rangoon. As group leader, I rode with them to the hotel, while the others followed in a bus. In the limousine Mr. Fleck asked if I had made any statements to the Burmese authorities in Akyab.

"Yes," I replied, concerned that perhaps I had done something wrong. "A colonel questioned me for an hour about the civil war in East Pakistan."

Mr. Fleck then reached into his vest pocket and handed me a paper. "Do you recognize this?" he asked. I began studying the poorly-typed paper when suddenly I realized that it was a copy of the interview just completed in Akyab. I wondered, *How in the world did this get into the hands of Mr. Fleck so quickly?* I have been duly impressed with the U.S. intelligence services ever since.

Mr. Hummel made certain that we were comfortably lodged in the Russian-built Inya Lake Hotel on the outskirts of Rangoon before leaving us. The first and most risky part of our journey was over on this 21st day of April. All of us were relieved that the evacuation had been successful and we were all safe. This news must now be communicated to relatives and friends all over the USA and Canada.

ASKING FOR THE MOON

*"For the Lord is a sun and shield: the Lord
will give grace and glory: No good thing will
be withhold form tham that walk uprightly."*
Psalm 84:11

My mind whirled as I pondered the events of the past several
days. I had already shared with Eleanor my restlessness and desire
to get back to the tribal people we had left behind. Would this be
possible? That question churned in my mind as I reviewed the
events of recent days.

Later that same evening after our arrival in Rangoon, Ambassador Hummel met with our group again stating that the Pakistan
government, now aware that 34 Americans had crossed into
Burma, were displeased. After all, according to their propaganda
and press releases to the outside world, life was normal and peace-
ful in East Pakistan. Why should foreigners evacuate? Mr.
Hummel shared this information with us because of a telegram he
had received from the Pakistan government. He felt that the
eventuality of our reentering East Pakistan looked very dim.

This news was troublesome and sobering. Before leaving that
evening, the ambassador agreed to help in any way he could and
to telex any communication that we wished to send.

After Mr. Hummel left, our group made two important decisions.
First, we would stick together as a group rather than break up and
scatter. From now on we would make ourselves known as the Malumghat Hospital Group. Secondly, I would begin immediately to

approach the Pakistan government officially on behalf of the group for permission to return to East Pakistan. We had left as a group, perhaps we could get back into the country more quickly as a group rather than as individuals.

The following morning I met with the ambassador to share the reasons behind our decisions. He readily agreed to telex our request to the Pakistan Foreign Ministry in Islamabad with copies to the Pakistan embassies in Islamabad and Bangkok for their information. The content of my letter contained these points:

1. That we left East Pakistan in obedience to the U.S. State Department's advice as announced on a VOA shortwave radio broadcast. It was not our desire to leave.

2. That we wanted to return to East Pakistan as soon as possible to take up our duties in the hospital and to continue our humanitarian services.

3. That our group of 34, including women and children, would wait in Bangkok, Thailand until that permission was granted.

The Burmese government, nervous about our controversial presence in Burma, allowed us to stay only two days in Rangoon before boarding us on a flight to Bangkok. Ambassador and Mrs. Hummel, Mr. Gene Martin, and Mr. Fleck were at the airport to see us off.

In Bangkok we booked lodging in the Christian and Missionary Alliance guest home on Pradipat Road. Bill and Bonnie Carlson, managers of the home, graciously found rooms for all and cared for us during the uncertain weeks that followed.

After settling in our temporary home, Mel Beals and I taxied directly to the American Embassy to report our arrival and seek assistance. The consul general, Mr. Wesley E. Jorgensen, received us graciously and indicated that he had already been alerted of our possible visit. We were pleased to learn that ambassador Hummel had followed through with his promise and had notified American and Pakistani embassies in southeast Asia. When Mr. Jorgensen asked how he might help us, I was ready.

"Sir," I said, "we evacuated from East Pakistan against our will and we want to return. I would like you to telex this information to the Foreign Ministry in Pakistan with copies to our embassies in Islamabad and Rangoon. Secondly, I would like you to introduce me to your Bangkok colleague, Pakistan's ambassador to Thailand. We need visas."

Mr. Jorgensen smiled and said, "Young man, you are asking for the moon. But," he added with a wide grin, "I believe if anybody can get it, you can!" He gave us his full cooperation.

When our group had evacuated from war-torn East Pakistan, most of us had visas which had already expired or were about to do so. We had been finding it increasingly difficult to obtain new visas in East Pakistan. Even when we were successful, they were valid for only one year, not for four years as in previous times. My purpose for meeting Pakistan's ambassador in Bangkok was to see if I could persuade him to renew our expired visas. Without question this was "asking for the moon." We had exited East Pakistan, illegally—according to his government—and he would surely have been apprised of that information by this time. Even I thought it would be ludicrous for him to renew our visas, but I would try. Nothing ventured, nothing gained!

The Pakistani ambassador, duly informed by Mr. Jorgensen of my visit, received me graciously. I proceeded to do what I knew how to do best. I smiled, shook hands, and talked about our pleasant and memorable experiences in his homeland, West Pakistan. I mentioned that my two oldest children were right then studying in Murree, West Pakistan, and that they loved living there. Then, getting to the business at hand, I explained our unfortunate circumstances; how we had been asked to leave the hospital in East Pakistan, and of our desire to return as soon as possible to reopen it. I also apprised him of our visa problems which needed to be solved before we could return.

Apparently favorably impressed, he picked up a phone and called the Third Secretary, ordering him to look into our visa situation. Before leaving the ambassador, I gave him copies of all my previous correspondence concerning our plans to return to East Pakistan and requested his help. He agreed to communicate our wishes to his superiors in Islamabad. We shook hands and he escorted me to the door.

The Third Secretary was Mr. Alam, a Bengali gentleman from Dhaka, East Pakistan. He was one of the few Bengali diplomats who had not yet defected to the newly proclaimed, but still illegal, government of Bangladesh. As I would soon learn, he was contemplating that decision. After a brief introduction, Mr. Alam glanced around nervously as if to make sure nobody was within hearing range. He lowered his voice and asked, "Are the reports true about what the Pakistan army is doing to my people in Bangladesh?"

His question opened the way for me to share the sad, but true, news of West Pakistan's oppressive military action, our evacuation story, and of our need for visas so we could return to the hospital. In those few short minutes we established a relationship that paid off handsomely. I pulled a stack of passports from an envelope and placed them on his desk. After carefully leafing through each one, he called his assistant. When a bearded West Pakistani man appeared in the doorway, Mr. Alam ordered him to issue new visas in all the passports.

I sat there holding my breath, praying silently, "*Lord, let the visas be stamped before something happens to retract his decision.*"

Shortly after the peon disappeared, I asked Mr. Alam if he was issuing us four-year, multiple-entry visas. "No," he replied. "Presently we are only issuing one-year visas."

I then hurriedly explained that our terms of service were for four years and it would be most helpful if we could get that kind of visa. He reached for his phone to call his assistant but found it busy. Slamming it down, he stepped out of the room, leaving me alone. Upon returning he said, "You are in luck. I caught my man just in time. Now you'll be receiving four-year visas." If there are such things as big and little miracles, this was a huge one! Our God was with us and working on our behalf. We missionaries met that evening for praise and prayer and a time of rejoicing for the overwhelming thing that God had done.

The wheels of diplomacy take time to work. Though we missionaries now possessed valid Pakistan visas, we had been told by Mr. Alam that we still needed *special* permission to re-enter war-torn East Pakistan; the military authorities there controlled who would or would not be admitted into Dhaka. One week after receiving our visas, I heard a rumor that travel restrictions to Dhaka had been lifted. I immediately went to the office of Pakistan International Airlines (PIA) to check it out. "You can't re-enter East Pakistan yet," they said, "but we have just reopened flights to West Pakistan. Those flights make a 45-minute layover in Dhaka for refueling and a custom's check before proceeding to Lahore."

Along with several others in the group, Eleanor and I had children studying at Murree Christian School in West Pakistan. Having learned that restrictions existed for travel there, I booked seats on PIA's first flight to Lahore via Dhaka. That flight was scheduled to depart from Bangkok on May 23, 1971, one month and two days after our evacuation through Burma.

Flight reservations in hand, I then cabled Reid Minich in Chittagong, hoping against all odds that he would receive it. We maintained a cable address in Chittagong, but it was questionable whether or not the system would be functioning. My cable detailed our travel plans and explained about the 45-minute stopover in Dhaka. I closed the message with, "Please notify Vic Olsen. Try to meet us."

An eerie, ghostly feeling prevailed as we disembarked in Dhaka for custom's clearance. The airport, usually crowded with people greeting or sending off relatives and friends, was empty except for gun-toting West Pakistani soldiers posted in key areas. While waiting for our luggage to be examined, I slipped away from the baggage area to see if Reid or one of the doctors had come. There, to my relief, standing behind a locked metal gate, was Dr. Vic Olsen. The cable message had gotten through and he had come to meet his wife, Joan. Miracle number five!

"Vic," I said hurriedly, "we have less than 45 minutes here before they fly us on to West Pakistan. We have new visas but no special permits to stay here."

"Tell Joan I'll be right back," he said as he turned and dashed away. "I'll see what I can do."

Customs officers were completing luggage inspection when Vic returned, a broad smile on his face. He had persuaded the Air Marshal to let us stay in Dhaka for 24 hours, until the next day's flight. That was miracle number six.

We spent that night with dear American friends, Mark and Ida Tucker, in Gulshan, a diplomatic enclave in Dhaka. But before retiring for the night, Vic and I planned a strategy for staying permanently. "Nothing ventured, nothing gained" applied in this case also.

In the morning we went directly to the man in charge of East Pakistan, General Rao Forman Ali Khan. At the Martial Law Headquarters located in the governor's mansion, we were ushered into the general's waiting room where Vic submitted a calling card. Shortly, the general called for us. After perfunctory greetings and handshakes, he asked how he might help us. He listened carefully as I related the evacuation drama and pointed out that his government had granted us new visas. Vic also made a strong and logical appeal as to why our missionaries should be allowed to return to the hospital at Malumghat. It had already been closed for a month and the people of the district were suffering. When we finished, the general clanged a desk bell. A peon appeared and was ordered to retrieve a file. After studying it for a few moments the general looked directly at me and asked, "Are you Mr. Walsh?" I was dumbfounded. *How did he know my name?* I realized then that copies of my correspondence to the Foreign Ministry in West

Pakistan from Rangoon and Bangkok had also reached East Pakistan.

Whether or not it was our entreaty, or the fact that we were Americans and the U.S. government was closely allied politically with Pakistan, the General agreed to let us stay. God answered our prayers with miracle number seven. Instead of flying to West Pakistan, the next day we flew south to Chittagong for a reunion with Reid Minich, Donn Ketcham and our national staff. The rest of our evacuation group flew in on Sunday, May 31. We were all safely home.

Word that we were back in Malumghat spread like wildfire. The "bamboo telegraph" worked beautifully. Tribal Christians from the Hill Tracts began arriving in delegations to welcome us back. What a joyful reunion and a time to make new plans for the future.

THE "FATHER OF THE NATION" RETURNS

"Render, therefore, to all their dues: tribute to
whom tribute is due; custom to whom custom;
fear to whom fear; honor to whom honor."
Romans 13:7

Sheik Mujibur Rahman had declared the independence of Bangladesh on March 26, 1971. Not until December 16, nearly nine months later, however, were the Pakistani generals forced to relinquish their grip on the land. From the time we re-entered the country on May 25 until December 16, we carried on our work, always wondering what the next day would bring. During those turbulent months, Bangladeshi young men, many of whom had earlier fled to neighboring India for refuge, engaged in guerrilla warfare against the occupying Pakistan army. We heard steady rumors of bridges and electric installations being blown up around the country. Reports also reached us of ships being sunk in Chittagong port by floating mines, daringly set adrift by the freedom fighters during the night. Month after month freedom fighter activity increased, making travel on the roads extremely risky.

In July, I flew to Dhaka to meet with a government official dealing with relief and rehabilitation activities in East Pakistan. I carried a request for him to allocate 25 tons of wheat to be used at our hospital in a "food for work" program. Many people living near the hospital, especially the Hindus whose homes had been destroyed by marauding military units, were suffering severe hardships.

As I sat in the Secretary's office, he called in another gentleman who introduced himself as Rolf G. Feiland, the Commercial Attaché of the West German embassy. A telephone rang while the three of us were visiting and the Secretary, excusing himself, left the room for a few minutes. I seized that opportunity to ask Mr. Feiland how he felt about the struggle going on in the country. Would the Bengali freedom fighters win? "No," he said optimistically, "the government's situation is improving. Pakistani troops will soon have everything under control. In fact, today I cabled my wife to rejoin me. She was evacuated to Frankfurt last March."

On a pessimistic note I replied, "I may be wrong, but my sources of information lead me to believe that the situation in the country is getting worse, not better, and that it will only be a matter of time before Bangladesh gains her independence." At that point the Secretary returned, ending the brief conversation.

Three days later in Chittagong, while eating lunch in a Chinese restaurant, I glanced at the daily newspaper. To my astonishment, on the front page I saw a picture of Mr. Feiland with this headline: GERMAN COMMERCIAL ATTACHÉ . . . KILLED IN A MINE BLAST. The article said that he had been driving outside the city of Dhaka when his vehicle hit a land mine and was blown to bits. The mine had been planted by Bangladeshi freedom fighters.

Guerrilla attacks like that one increased throughout the country until December when the freedom fighters, assisted by an invasion of the sympathetic Indian army, were victorious. History now records December 16, 1971 as that special day.

Those final hours before Victory Day brought tense moments for those of us at Malumghat. An Indian Air Force plane circling above the hospital dropped two bombs which exploded with a deafening roar a half-mile away. Parents dashed to rescue the petrified missionary children who were in school at the time. Eleanor and I huddled in a bathroom with our kids until the danger was over.

At first we thought the lone bomber was targeting the hospital. Later we learned that the local community center, which had a wireless antenna protruding from its roof, was the actual target. After firing a final air-to-surface missile at the same building, the plane circled and disappeared. The missile failed to explode and the bombs missed their target, leaving behind two huge craters.

On December 17, the day after liberation, reports reached us of the slaughter that had taken place in Chittagong by the retreating non-Bengalis. I drove the 65 miles to the city to see for myself what had happened. Both wailing and jubilation filled the air. Grieving people, seeing this foreigner in their midst, pleaded with me to look into septic tanks filled with skeletons and decomposing bodies. At one check post where Pakistani sentries had done guard duty, I counted dozens of human skulls, Bengali people who had been executed during the preceding months.

What irony, I thought. *West Pakistani Muslims killing their East Pakistani brothers!*

The tragedy and suffering that the Bengali people had endured faded slightly when the international press reported that Sheik Mujibur Rahman, the hero of Bangladesh, was to be released from prison in Pakistan and would soon return to join his people.

I was in Dhaka on January 10, 1972 when the "father of the nation" arrived. The capital buzzed with excitement as a now independent people with a newly-gained freedom waited for their hero. Millions of people filled the streets. Police were stationed along the parade route from the airport to central Dhaka where the Sheik, an eloquent orator, would give a victory speech.

Since I was in Dhaka, I decided it would be worth the effort to be at the airport when he landed. Although official permission to enter would be difficult to obtain, I did try—only to find the office closed. Proceeding on the premise that it would be easier to ask forgiveness than to get permission, I decided to try my luck. International Christian Fellowship missionary Phil Parshall agreed to drive me to the airport.

A quarter of a mile from the airport, police diverted all traffic onto side streets in a determined effort to control the excited public. At that point I left Phil and walked the rest of the way. I didn't know exactly where I would first encounter security police, but I had made myself look as official as possible wearing a tie and blazer, two cameras slung around my neck and my social security card fastened to my lapel. Stuffing a newspaper into my coat pocket, I headed straight for the airport's main entrance which was flanked by armed soldiers. Moving with a determined gait, looking neither to the right nor to the left, I walked unchallenged past the guards, through the main terminal building to the tarmac, where hundreds of VIP's, police, party officials, and members of the world press were assembled.

A speaker's podium had been installed on the tarmac with a red carpet extending to the point where the British Royal Air Force (RAF) jet would taxi to a halt. The Sheik was arriving from London because the Pakistan government had refused to allow him to fly directly from Pakistan to liberated Bangladesh.

Waiting for the plane presented a problem for me. The idea of being asked to leave didn't appeal to me. Other reporters and newsmen, in their efforts to kill time, were making acquaintances and visiting with one another, a courtesy I wanted to avoid. I moved around the fringes of the crowd hoping to remain anonymous, but my luck ran out when an Asian reporter, in a friendly mood, approached and asked which press I was representing. Thinking quickly I replied, "The Baptist Press. We publish articles for the Christian community." Satisfied, he dropped that subject and we engaged in small talk. I stuck with my new friend to avoid having to repeat my story to someone else. (Actually, I have published numerous articles and authored the book *Ripe Mangoes* with the Regular Baptist Press, but I wasn't under their auspices that day.)

At last, the plane carrying Sheik Mujib appeared in the sky above us. An eerie silence fell on the tarmac as all eyes turned upward. I caught the pent-up emotion of that moment in the face of a policeman standing at attention beside me. Head tilted toward the sky, huge tears trickled down his face. The hero of Bangladesh had come home.

As the plane landed and taxied closer, pandemonium broke out. Celebrating crowds surged forward, making it dangerous for the pilot to reach the planned terminal point. Finally, the plane stopped and the door slid open. When Sheik Mujib appeared in the plane's doorway, the crowd exploded. Mujib's feet never touched the red carpet as he was buoyed along on the shoulders of political cronies and well-wishers. One after another, dignitaries hung flower leis around his neck which he, from time to time, cast off because of the weight. Finally, his hair disheveled and glasses askew, he was carried to the podium. Unable to quiet the jubilant celebration, Sheik Mujhib was hoisted to the bed of a decorated truck to lead the parade to Ramna Park in central Dhaka.

I stood watching the parade vehicles lining up behind Mujib's truck, wondering how to get back to the hotel, when a military officer invited me to ride in his jeep. As it turned out, I rode proudly and comfortably in the second vehicle behind the truck that carried the infant nation's founding father and first president.

One mile and one hour later, when our jeep finally reached the Intercontinental Hotel near Ramna Park, I smiled, saluted the officers, and jumped off, cameras still dangling from my neck. I had just witnessed history in the making, participating in one of Golden Bengal's unforgettable moments.

Later it was my privilege, along with Bob Adolph and Vic Olsen, to have a private audience with Sheik Mujibur Rahman. I shall never forget his pleased reaction when I spoke with him in Bengali, his native tongue. He smiled broadly and said, "You have learned Bengali. Good!" Both of us were well aware that it was a Bengali language dispute with Pakistan that lay at the root of the revolution.

Sadly, on August 15, 1975, four years after his triumphal entry, Sheik Mujibur Rahman, the hero of the independence movement and father of the new nation called Bangladesh, was gunned down, along with most of his immediate family members, in a bloody military coup.

During that politically unstable year of 1975, while I was on furlough, the tribal work continued to prosper under the leadership of colleagues David Totman and George Weber. In a Tribal Committee report dated October 1975, George wrote: "Over the past year we have seen an increase in the tribal work at Hebron and Malumghat. More men have been hired as evangelists, more training classes have been established and more areas are being reached with the gospel. The tribal work has been divided. Malumghat will serve the tribal peoples south of the Matamahari River and Hebron will work north of the river.

"The evangelists have preached in dozens of villages. A number of those meetings were return visits to build up the believers, to prepare some for baptism and to baptize others. There have also been professions of faith in the Marma tribe. There is a need for more work among those people.

"A new opportunity has arisen for work with the Chakmas, the largest, the most advanced, and the most prestigious of the tribes. A cousin of the present Chakma king, after a serious motorcycle injury, was brought to the hospital. He and his mother have become believers. Before returning to their home in Rangamati they said, 'There is now every chance of a movement for Christ developing among our Chakma people. If you will help us, guide us, and advise us, there is no reason why this should not happen.'"

The year 1975 was not only a tumultuous year politically in Bangladesh, it was also a year of spiritual victories within the tribes of the Chittagong Hill Tracts.

CHAPTER 20

THE TRIBAL "PEACE CORPS"

"In perils in the city, in perils in the wilderness . . ."
1 Corinthians 11:26

Many different ethnic tribal groups live in the Chittagong Hill Tracts. Chakmas, Bawms, Pankhos, Lushais, Khyangs, Chaks, Kumis, Tipperahs, Marmas (also called Moghs), and Murungs are some of them. These minority groups differ from the majority lowland Bengali people in several respects: they are Oriental in their physical features, most claim to be adherents of either the Hindu, Buddhist or animistic religions, and they practice the slash-and-burn method of cultivation.

The Bengali people, on the other hand, are of Indian racial stock and are followers of the Muslim, Hindu, and Buddhist religions. They farm traditionally, plowing rice paddies with cows or water buffalo. Both the tribals and Bengalis have one thing in common: all are rice eaters. But, as is often the case in mixed populations, there is no love lost between them.

After the brief war in 1965 closed the Chittagong Hill Tracts to missionary travel, tribal evangelists and pastors came to us for training and fellowship. They then returned to the hills to minister to their own people. Although we missed the joy of visiting their villages, the enforced indigenous approach has proven to be extremely effective. The tribal church continues to grow without our physical presence in their villages.

In recent years, however, Bangladesh's overpopulation problem has severely strained the relationship between the government and the tribal people, and greatly affected our work. In 1960 when Eleanor and I first arrived in Bangladesh, a country the size of Wisconsin, the population was 45 million. A 1998 statistic quotes approximately 140 million. With the country's population increasing, but its land area remaining the same, the government decided to allow landless Bengali families to settle in the Chittagong Hill Tracts. That seemed reasonable from the government's point of view because less than one percent of the country's population occupied one-tenth of the country's land mass. But that change of policy created an ongoing problem.

The resettlement process started slowly in the middle 1980's, but has increased since then. The Bengali incursion into the hills was, as one might expect, upsetting to the tribal peoples. We missionaries became aware of this when tribal Christians began reporting, with increasing frequency, conflicts with the new settlers who began to forcefully occupy tribal farmlands and cut their forests. It was only a matter of time until tribal leaders grouped to resist the invasion. When political negotiations proved unsuccessful, tribal leaders formed a guerrilla organization called the *Shanti Bahini* (Peace Corps) to fight for their rights.

After setting up a shadow government, tribal leaders began to levy taxes on their people, one of which was called the "*jubok/juboti*" tax, meaning a taxation of the young men and young women. Those revenues were used to purchase weapons from India and Burma.

The *Shanti Bahini* also moved from village to village recruiting young people to become either freedom fighters or fund raisers. As one would expect, such activities began to affect the Christian youth and raised a question about their loyalties. Should they, as

Bangladeshi citizens, be loyal to their government or to their *Shanti Bahini* leaders? They were caught on the horns of a dilemma which is vividly expressed in the Bengali language as finding one-self "between the alligator in the river and the tiger on the shore." If they joined the *Shanti Bahini* they would be in trouble with the Bangladesh government. If they refused to join, they would be in trouble with the *Shanti Bahini*. Moral and ethical conflicts arose because we had taught the Christians, according to the Scriptures, to be subject to the government in authority over them. Their dilemma still exists today.

A pattern of *Shanti Bahini* activity soon developed. Encroaching Bengali settlers would be kidnapped and never heard from again. Occasionally, government officials would be kidnapped and held for ransom. Once several foreigners representing an oil explo-ration company were kidnapped. A huge ransom was paid for their release. As time went on, it became easy for the *Shanti Bahini* to extort money from Bengali merchants living near the border of the Hill Tracts district. A simple note to a shop owner to send money "or else" usually did the trick.

Eventually, the *Shanti Bahini* movement became a problem for the hospital. Tribal Christians who worked for us became suspect, either as being rebels or sympathizers. If they were suspect, then we missionaries were, too. Officials from the National Security Intelligence (NSI) made periodic visits to inquire about our activ-ities. "Is the hospital supplying medicines to tribal guerrillas?" was an often-asked question. Of course we would never knowingly do such a thing, we reported.

As Christians working in Bangladesh, missionaries sympathized with the government's population problem and, at the same time, to the encroachment problem the tribal people faced. We were also aware that overt expressions of loyalty to our tribal friends could cause a lot of trouble. We had to exercise caution to protect ourselves both from the government and the *Shanti Bahini*. Our mission policy has always been to remain totally neutral in political matters. But as individuals, it was easy to form opinions about issues, especially when they affected our ministries.

Shanti Bahini activity had always seemed rather distant to us, occurring miles away in the border areas. Then, in 1985, Bengali timber merchants began logging in the forests near Memorial Christian Hospital. After that it was only a matter of time before the tribal guerrillas moved in to collect "taxes." They were successful in their efforts. A local truck driver told me that all Bengali truck owners had to pay 5,000 takas ($175) each for permission to operate in the logging zone. We heard of at least two who didn't pay; those trucks were seized and burned.

My unexpected encounter with *Shanti Bahini* guerrillas occurred early one morning in March. Up at dawn, I told Eleanor I was taking a short drive to see if I could bag a couple of wild chickens. "I'll be back at 7:00 for breakfast," I promised.

Wild chickens often exited the forest at dawn to graze along the main road before traffic started moving. I frequently took advantage of this opportunity to shoot a few. On that March morning I drove out the hospital gate and turned north toward an army encampment three miles away. That three-mile stretch of road winds through forests where I had often seen jungle chickens. As I rounded a bend, I saw a brilliantly colored rooster and several hens on the road in front of me. Inching slowly forward within shooting range, I shot the rooster, which I retrieved and laid on the floor near my feet. *Great luck!* I thought, as I turned and headed toward home.

Before reaching the hospital, however, I decided on the spur of the moment to turn into a logging road called the Accra Road, so-named because a large contingent of African soldiers had camped there during World War II. That rutted road, which I often used for hunting, winds its way eastward into the Hill Tracts. Perhaps I could get one more chicken before breakfast.

As I turned the car, two men dressed in military camouflage suddenly stepped out of the jungle and stopped me. They were armed, one with a sten gun, the other with a rifle. In a split second, even before my adrenaline had time to activate, I recognized them as *Shanti Bahini* guerrillas. I had heard about them for years, now they were confronting me.

"Who are you?" the leader asked gruffly through the window in the Chittagonian dialect. "What are you doing here?" Those were easy questions.

Nervously I replied, "I am a missionary working at the Memorial Christian Hospital at Malumghat. I came this morning to hunt wild chickens. They make good curry." Saying this, I reached for the dead rooster and showed it to them.

"Here, you can have it," I offered. They weren't interested. Then, looking at my watch, I said, "I have to be going now. I have important duty at the hospital and must be back by 7:00 a.m." The leader of the group, the one holding a sten gun, turned and began talking with other men hidden in the jungle. After a brief conversation with them, he rounded the passenger side of the car, and crawled in. His partner struggled into the back seat with his long rifle. The leader then motioned for me to start driving.

The gravity of the situation impressed me. There I was, totally helpless, driving a little Toyota Corolla deeper into the jungle with armed guerrillas. I thought of Eleanor who, by this time, was expecting me home for breakfast. Could I talk myself out of this predicament? One thing was certain: the Lord had allowed it to happen; I would trust Him for rescue. I drove slowly for about two miles on the rutted road before dirt and brush began scraping the bottom of the car. Fearing a punctured oil pan, I told the commander that we must stop or the car would be damaged. He forced me to go several hundred yards more before signaling me to halt. Then my uninvited guests got out and walked away, leaving me alone.

My first thought was to turn the car around quickly and make a speedy getaway. I dropped that as an option because there was no convenient place to turn. Besides, just because I couldn't see them didn't mean they weren't watching me, and I would never see Eleanor again with a bullet in my back! With those thoughts in mind I decided it best to remain a live coward than become a dead hero. I did, however, take the opportunity to hide my gun and ammunition in the trunk of the car, hoping they would forget I had them. *Out of sight, out of mind*, I reasoned.

A short time later the men returned and ordered me to turn the car around. I was relieved because we were now heading in the direction where they had arrested me, near the main highway. I began telling them about the hospital and my love for the tribal people. I informed them that I had already learned the Tipperah language and was concerned about tribal problems in general. For emphasis I added, "If I had my way and could obtain government permission, I'd be spending much more time in your beautiful hills."

Having gotten their attention, I changed the subject and asked them to keep a lookout for wild chickens; the one I had bagged wasn't enough for a good meal. At this, they began craning their necks in each direction.

On reaching the spot where I had been arrested, the leader ordered me to stop. When we got out of the car, he shouted a command and three more armed men appeared, one carrying a backpack. After more conversation the backpacker reached in his bag and brought out a package of cookies. The leader, ripping it open, handed me one and took one for himself.

I thought, *If I have to die it won't be on an empty stomach!*

I felt, however, that the gesture of offering food was friendly and meant they wouldn't harm me. I was a friend, not an enemy, and they knew it. After eating the cookie, I pointed to my watch again and told them that I really had important duty at the hospital. At this, the leader told me to go. Relieved, I started the car and began to pull away when he stopped me yet again. *Oh, no*, I wondered. *What now?*

"Do you have any buckshot?" the commander asked.

Fearing the worst, I thought, *Will they take away my gun?* I stopped the engine and cracked opened the trunk just enough to reach in my hand and retrieve the bag of ammunition which he dumped on the ground. After pawing through the contents, he kept five rounds of buckshot—all that I had with me.

At that point he asked if I would drive him to Chittagong.

"Chittagong?" I queried. "The army would catch you at one of their many check posts."

"Oh, I wouldn't travel in these clothes," he said. "I would be dressed like you."

"No problem," I said. "I make monthly trips to Chittagong. I'll get in touch with you when I go. Tell me how to reach you." With that proposal I had put the ball in his court and, obviously not wishing to reveal any secrets, he dropped the subject and motioned for me to go.

Eleanor was patiently waiting when I returned for a late breakfast. I wrestled briefly with whether or not to tell her—or anyone—what had happened. The news might be too upsetting. But, deciding it best to be open, I told my story and later shared it with our colleagues. The events of that morning had drained me emotionally. Grateful for the Lord's protection, I went back to bed and fell into a deep sleep.

The next day, I felt it important to report my experience to the local police and to the local army colonel. The colonel listened with rapt attention because he made daily trips past the Accra Road. Concerned about his own safety he asked, "Do you have any advice for me?"

"Yes," I replied, "Avoid traveling early in the morning or late at night. You should also vary your travel schedule so as not to reveal a pattern."

"Thanks," he said, "that's good advice. Thank you very much."
And he really meant it.

Several days after my capture I received a note from the *Shanti
Bahini* commander, delivered by a known tribal Christian, assuring
me that they would not harm me or any of the hospital personnel.
That was good news.

The *Shanti Bahini* are still active in the Chittagong Hill Tracts.
Even after periodic negotiations with government officials, the
tribal people have yet to obtain a satisfactory solution to their
grievances. I often wonder if they will ever prevail or if, one day,
like the North American Indians, they will be driven from their
ancestral lands or be forced onto reservations.

In May 1994, a Bangladeshi friend and leader, Mr. Mominul
Hoque Chowdhury, representing the local Bengali people,
unveiled a monument in my honor and in honor of the Accra
Road troops who died during the Second World War. This was
his way of expressing his deep gratitude for my friendship as a
brother in Christ, and for my years of service in Bangladesh. The
inscription, inlaid in marble, reads:

ACCRA ROAD
This memorial is for the gallant soldiers of the
"GOLD COAST DIVISION"
Who laid down their lives in the Second World War
and whose camp was three miles east of this point on the
Accra Road, so named in memory of their home capital.
Inaugurated this 13th day of May, 1994 by:
Rev. D.J. WALSH
Chairman of the Memorial Christial Hospital
who loved and served this country for 35 years.
Courtesy of: Mominul Hoque Chowdhury (Dulahazara)

CHAPTER 21

DILEMMAS, PROBLEMS, AND OBSTACLES

"Blessed are ye, when men shall revile you, and
persecute you, and shall say all manner of evil
against you falsely, for my sake. Rejoice, and
be exceeding glad: for great is your reward in
heaven: for so persecuted they the prophets
which were before you."
Matthew 5:11

Whenever you work with people, you inevitably find yourself involved in their problems. This was certainly true with the tribal people of Bangladesh. Many of their problems stem from natural causes, others from their enemies. We have also been keenly aware of Satan's attacks on faithful Christians who have turned from idols to serve the true and living God.

Early in our time at Hebron many Tipperahs sought loans for purchasing seed rice which they needed for their new crops. We wanted to help them even though we were hampered by limited financial resources. Because of their urgent need, we devised a plan to assist them with low-interest loans which they would repay at harvest time. In that way we could establish an ongoing, revolving loan fund to cope with future emergencies.

When news spread that we were issuing loans, dozens of tribals descended on Hebron from all directions seeking money. A bit upset and concerned, I asked evangelist Ancherai why they were coming.

"Normally," he explained, "after a rice harvest, each family sets aside enough seed for next season's planting." That made good sense to me.

"Why, then," I asked, "are they coming for loans now?"

"Haven't you heard?" he asked. "The rats destroyed most of last year's crop, forcing the people to eat their seed rice to stay alive. Having eaten their seed rice, they need money now to purchase new seed."

Ancherai went on to explain that a rat plague occurs in the hills at 50-year intervals. During that 50th year a new crop of flowering bamboo produces a profusion of seeds which attracts and increases the rat population. Some believe there is also a chemical reaction that increases their fertility. Regardless, hordes of rats can destroy a standing rice crop in one night. One Tipperah man told of the time he left his acre of rice in the evening only to return in the morning to find it gone, straw and all. The rats had snipped off each rice stalk near the ground, dragging it away into crevices and holes in the hillsides.

Helping our tribal friends with loans proved to be a mixed blessing. Experience soon taught us that it is much easier to dispense money than to collect it. Invariably people faced new problems the following year, then sought to have their loans dismissed.

We later learned that the main reason for approaching us for loans was to avoid the local *mohajons* (money lenders) who charged interest—usury would be more accurate—at the rate of 10% per month, requiring gold and silver jewelry as a security deposit. No wonder the tribal people tried us first.

Missionaries working in Bangladesh continually face the "loan" problem. Hardly a day passes without someone asking for financial help. There is no easy solution when working among the poorest of the poor.

The reality of Ancherai's rat story hit home one morning as I crossed a rice field and noticed children on their knees. Each rice paddy is surrounded by an aisle, approximately one foot wide and one foot high, which serves to retain rain water during the monsoon season as well as to demarcate lines of ownership. That field of rice had already been harvested. Curious, I found each child walking along the aisles with a basket containing heads of rice.

"Where are you getting the rice?" I asked.

"In these holes," they replied. Then a small girl, pointing to a hole in the aisle in front of her, inserted her slender hand and drew out a sheaf of rice—rice that the rats had put in storage. *Another way of gleaning,* I concluded.

Rats were not the only problem. One day a group of Tipperah believers arrived at Hebron from Chimpru village, concern written on their faces. After the customary greetings I asked, "What's the trouble? You look worried."

Ramoni, their leader, replied, "I am in trouble and I urgently need a loan for 2,000 *takas*" (approximately $200—a small fortune at that time).

"That's a huge amount. Why so much?" I asked.

"The police are threatening a murder case against me unless I pay them that much," he replied.

Ramoni told us his story. His aged mother had accidentally fallen from the verandah of his house, built on stilts high off the ground. She never regained consciousness and died from the impact. "So what's the problem?" I asked. "How did the police get involved?"

"A Satan worshiper," he explained, "an enemy of us Christians, falsely reported to the police that I pushed my mother off the verandah because she was old and had become a liability. The police came for an inquiry and left again. I thought no more of it until today when they returned demanding money, or else."

This is extortion, pure and simple! I thought. *I can't let that happen.*

Ramoni had brought a delegation with him because, according to Tipperah custom, they would have to help financially if I didn't. Although I hurt for their problem, I told them there were two reasons why I couldn't loan them money. First, I didn't have that much, and secondly, if they paid the police, it would appear that Ramoni had, indeed, committed the crime. Instead, I wrote a letter which I asked them to deliver to the Officer-in-Charge (O.C.) of the police station. I simply stated that Ramoni and his villagers were members of the Christian community, and that Ramoni was a man of good character whom I had known for many years. In conclusion, I requested to be notified if there was a case and, if so, that I wanted to be present as a character witness.

Some weeks later I saw Ramoni in the Lama bazaar and asked what had happened.

"I gave the O.C. your letter," he said, "and the police haven't bothered us since."

A more serious situation developed on another occasion. From time to time Mongsing, a Christian boy of the Khyong tribe, came from his home east of Chittagong to visit relatives and to hunt wild boar in the jungles near our hospital. One day, after a weekend of hunting, he hopped on a bus to return home. When the driver stopped for gasoline along the way, someone reported to the police that a tribal person was on board. They police arrived immediately to interrogate him, suspecting that he might be a member of the outlawed *Shanti Bahini*. While searching his shoulder bag they found several rounds of shotgun ammunition but no gun license. Their suspicions confirmed, they arrested Mongsing and marched him off to the police station where he was beaten and further interrogated about his activities. Although he told the truth about hunting with his uncle's gun, they refused to believe him. He was charged with illegal possession of ammunition and sent to jail in Chittagong to await a hearing. If convicted, as he surely would be, the law demanded seven years of rigorous imprisonment.

Several months later, Mongsing's uncle, Leslie Gonsalves, who worked at our hospital, sought my help. He reported that Mongsing's case would be tried in Patiya, a district court near the place of his arrest. Leslie begged me to attend the trial and I agreed.

Arriving at the courthouse early on the day of the trial, we saw hundreds of people milling about the courtyard, waiting for their cases to be heard. We went first to a special room where public *pleaders* (lawyers) were available for hire. Leslie hired one of the brighter looking ones to represent Mongsing and to draft the necessary defense papers.

A short time later, a paddy wagon from the Chittagong prison drove into the compound. When the vehicle stopped, Mongsing peered out of a barred window, looking as frightened as a trapped animal. When he spotted us, an ever-so-slight smile of relief crept over his face. He knew he had friends in that hostile crowd.

Leslie and I had a short session with the lawyer before the case was called. A policeman led the shackled boy to a docket in front of the judge who sat, Buddha-like, in his black robe. I pushed my way into the crowded courtroom, already filling with curiosity seekers. The judge had no sooner begun questioning Mongsing when he spotted me. The only foreigner present, I was highly visible. Acting nervous, he stopped and asked in broken English, "Why you are here? Can I help you something?"

"Yes," I replied, "I have come to testify on behalf of that young boy who is a friend of my family."

The judge called me forward and ordered his secretary to record my testimony. I told the court that I had known Mongsing from childhood, that he had grown up with our son Phillip, and that he had come to Malumghat for hunting. He was returning home by bus when he was falsely accused of being a member of the *Shanti Bahini* and arrested. I further explained that the ammunition he carried was from my personal supply, and that he was saving it for his next hunting trip. Closing my statement, I assured the judge that Mongsing was not a member of the outlawed *Shanti Bahini* and that he was a Christian and a Bangladeshi citizen. I would stand good for his bail.

After the judge dismissed me, Leslie and I left the courtroom to wait for a judgment. Minutes later I felt a tug on my arm. The judge's peon said, "Come. His Honor wishes to see you in his private chamber."

I followed the peon to a room adjacent to the courtroom. The judge, having declared a recess, was sitting in a chair waiting for me. He stood as I entered, shook hands, and offered me a chair. After ordering the peon to bring tea, we sat down.

"Where are you from?" he asked.

"Memorial Christian Hospital, Malumghat."

"You love that boy, don't you?" he reasoned.

"If I didn't, I wouldn't be here today." I replied. "I know he is innocent of the charges. That's why I've put my reputation at stake and have come here today."

At this juncture he surprised me. "Your Jesus loved people, too, didn't He? I've read about Him in your Christian holy book. That's why you love this boy, isn't it?"

His question opened a witnessing opportunity and I zeroed in with the gospel message. He listened patiently for a short time then suddenly changed the subject.

"I have a medical problem," he confided. With that, he pulled up a pant leg and showed me his leg which was covered with ugly looking scales. *Eczema?* I wondered. But how was I to know? Obviously, he thought I was a doctor and that I could help.

After inspecting his leg with measured interest, I asked for a sheet of paper. During the next few minutes I carefully logged his medical history before suggesting that he see a specialist at our hospital.

"I will make an appointment for you." I offered.

Satisfied, he blurted out, "I'm granting bail for that boy. You can take him now. I will lose his file and there will be no case."

Mongsing was one happy boy. I was one happy "doctor," and Leslie was one grateful uncle.

During our years in Bangladesh we were able to overcome many difficult situations because of the reputation of the Memorial Christian Hospital. Seeing the hospital logo on my calling card, government officials often wanted to discuss their medical problems. Though not a doctor, I learned to make prudent referrals. I often joke about my medical knowledge. I have only two prescriptions: for any pain above the waist, aspirin; any pain below the waist, laxatives.

Another complicated problem arose one day when a group of frightened Tipperahs came to me.

"Sahib," their spokesman said. "last night the Shanti Bahini burst into Pastor Gonachandra's house looking for his nephew, Butiram. When he obediently showed them the room where the young man was sleeping, one of the intruders jarred him awake with a hard kick. As Butiram sat up, half asleep and dazed, another man pulled a pistol and shot him dead before the pastor's eyes."

Probing further into their story they reported that the Shanti Bahini were angry with Butiram because he had taken employment as a teacher in a government school instead of joining their ranks. They considered him to be a government collaborator.

The delegation also informed me that the police, upon receiving news of the shooting, arrested Gonachandra because someone had falsely reported him as a supporter of the outlawed Shanti Bahini. I could see the frustration on their faces and promised that I would try to help their pastor.

Pastor Gonachandra is a little man, barely five feet tall, who suffers from asthma. Several years earlier he had been converted to Christ through the preaching of evangelist Ancherai. Although illiterate, he has a deep love for the Lord and the Word of God, portions of which he has memorized. Like Ancherai, Gonachandra has an evangelist's heart and boldly tries to win his fellow Tipperahs to Christ. Months after his arrest Gonachandra learned that it was the district Tipperah headman, a powerful but wicked man to whom he had been witnessing, who had made the false report to the police that resulted in Gonachandra's arrest.

For nearly three years Gonachandra suffered in a rat-infested prison before we found an opportunity to help him. During that time he was beaten, endured electric shock treatments, and lived on food barely fit for animals. Furthermore, he was imprisoned without the benefit of a trial. His wife and children sold all of their livestock and most of their land in efforts to get him released on bail, but without success.

One day the General Officer Commanding (GOC) of the Chittagong Division of the army came to the hospital with a medical problem. After caring for him, Dr. Donn Ketcham and other members of the staff entertained him at a special tea. When the general left that day he said, "If I can ever be of help to you, please feel free to call on me."

Hearing this report from Donn, I immediately thought of Gonachandra suffering in the Chittagong jail. The military police had arrested him and put him there. I knew he had been falsely accused, but was also aware of the political ramifications involving the illegal *Shanti Bahini*. Still, I suggested to Donn that this might be the time to try for Gonachandra's release. Donn agreed. We composed a letter to the GOC and sent it off with a prayer.

Several weeks later I heard a rap on our door. There, to my amazement, stood Pastor Gonachandra! He was grinning from ear to ear as we hugged each other. Sitting together drinking tea, he shared the story of his release, then pulled an official document from his shoulder bag and handed it to me. It had been signed by the GOC. God had honored our efforts and answered our prayers.

That evening the tribal Christians staged a special thanksgiving feast for Gonachandra and the missionaries. After the meal I asked him to share his testimony with the group. He stood quietly for a minute, and after gaining his composure said, "I'm extremely happy to be here with you tonight. I never thought I would see you again. I've suffered much during these past three years, yet God has been with me. During my time in prison, I led another prisoner, one of our fellow Tipperahs, to the Lord. He'll be coming to me for baptism as soon as he's released."

Gonachandra continued, "My experience tonight is like that of the woman mentioned in John 16:21. 'A woman when she is in travail hath sorrow, because her hour is come: but as soon as she is delivered of the child, she remembereth no more the anguish, for joy that a man is born into the world.' That's the way I feel tonight. I've forgotten my sorrows because of the joy I have in seeing you again."

That special man of God had the wonderful privilege of baptizing the man he had won to the Lord in prison. Later the wicked headman who had falsely reported him to the military police also came to know Christ and was baptized. Gonachandra, though now old and physically weak, is still serving his Lord as a village pastor.

Over the years we not only have had the privilege of winning people to Christ, but also suffering vicariously with them when they were suffering and then extending ourselves to help them when they were distressed and in trouble.

HARVEST IN THE HILLS

"Verily, verily, I say unto you, except a corn
of wheat fall into the ground and die, it abideth
alone: but if I die, it bringeth forth much fruit."
John 12:24

I watched that day as tribal Christians from all over the Chittagong Hill Tracts descended on Hebron. On December 5, 1989 55 Christian leaders representing 55 village churches came together to form an official fellowship: an association of churches. Doing so would not only benefit their future spiritual development but also give them organizational identity in the eyes of the government.

The first person to sign that historic document was Pastor Gonachandra Tipperah, that illiterate but saintly man of God who had innocently suffered a three-year prison term in a Chittagong jail. He firmly pressed his thumbprint to the document, smiling from ear to ear.

As missionary patriarch of the tribal ministry, and guest of honor at the organizational ceremony, I had the unique privilege of witnessing the signing of the document and addressing the group. I reviewed the highlights of our years among them, recalling Rev. Barnard's prayer uttered in the Chittagong cemetery. I spoke also of Paul Miller and Harry Goehring and the sacrifices they had made for the tribal people. Surely the group seated on bamboo mats before me represented the fruit for which those missionaries had so fervently prayed. I challenged them to consider what their newly formed fellowship could mean for Christ in the future.

Representing ABWE that day was George Collins, the young missionary who married our Debra, the daughter who gave us such a scare on the *Hellenic Splendor* in 1960. George met Debbie in college in 1976. Appointed to missionary service by ABWE, they arrived in Bangladesh in 1983. After language study, George assumed responsibility for the tribal work with a goal to see it nationalized by 1994, if not earlier. In the field council's opinion, and taking into consideration the government's policy to reduce foreign missionary presence in Bangladesh, the time had come to turn over the work, giving tribal leaders control of their own future.

Gunijon Tipperah, evangelist Ancherai's protégé, co-chaired the meeting with George. Gunijon, like Robichandro and Ancherai, had lived in Duniram Village as a child. He vividly remembers the day in 1962 when two white strangers, missionaries, visited his village. Their appearance frightened him as he clung to his father's leg. He was too young to even think that one day he would grow up and work with those same men.

Gunijon's mother, a Chakma, deserted the family when he was four years old. Shortly thereafter, his father contracted leprosy and moved his family to the Chittagong Hill Tract town of Chandragona where the Baptist Missionary Society operated the Arthington Memorial Hospital and Leprosarium. There, under the watchful eyes of British missionaries Dr. & Mrs. Michael Flowers, Gunijon attended the mission school through the sixth grade. The Flowerses, observing Gunijon's eagerness to learn, provided funds for him to attend the Baptist High School at Barisal in central Bangladesh.

In 1967 while Gunijon was at Barisal, his father, now cured of leprosy, obtained a gardener's job at our Memorial Christian Hospital. One day in 1969, while visiting his father, Gunijon attended a hospital prayer meeting where he heard Dr. Vic Olsen give a lesson on John 3:16.

"For God so loved the world, that he gave his only begotten Son, that whosoever believeth in him should not perish, but have everlasting life."

That message pierced his heart. Before returning to Barisal, Gunijon made the great faith decision to trust Christ as his personal Savior and Lord. A year later, after graduating from high school, he returned to Malumghat where he was baptized.

In 1970 Gunijon began attending the annual Bible conferences at Hebron, where he associated with evangelist Ancherai and began traveling with him on preaching tours. Ancherai's love and zeal for the Lord greatly impressed the young man. Those preaching tours, and my challenging him to consider giving his life to serve his people, eventually bore fruit.

One day Gunijon sat meditating under a *shishu* tree at Hebron with the thought on his mind, *If Ancherai should pass away, would I be able to take his place? Would I be able to preach with his zeal?* That very day, after heart searching and prayer, he dedicated his life to serve his Lord as zealously as did evangelist Ancherai. A few years later, on August 4, 1978, Ancherai's mantle fell heavily upon Gunijon's shoulders.

Since its inception in 1989, the tribal association has doubled in size to more than 110 village churches. Pastor Gunijon is chairman of the association which has a seven member supervisory board. One of those board members is my namesake, a young man named Awshai Tipperah whose evangelist father, Robichandro, named him after me. I have always been known to the Tipperahs as "Walsh Sahib" or "Awshai" as they pronounce it. This educated young man not only serves the tribal association but is also the principal of the Chittagong branch of the Bible Correspondence School.

Hebron, that special two-thirds of an acre, searched out and purchased by the founding ABWE missionaries in Bangladesh, has expanded over the years to more than 14 acres. It has become the tribal association's center for education and evangelism. Today, in addition to numerous schools established in the villages, Hebron houses a boarding school with facilities to educate more than 100 resident students. Young people from the different tribes are learning to read and write which, in turn, gives them access to the great treasury of Christian tracts and books already available in Bangladesh.

Leaders from each of the tribes have residences at Hebron. From that ideal hub they reach out to their own people. They have purchased property in different locations which will eventually become headquarters for their individual tribes. In time we foresee each tribe forming its own fellowship of churches, as the tribal leaders evangelize and educate their own people.

Hebron also continues to host the annual tribal Bible conference. George Collins built a sturdy pavilion to accommodate the conference, which has grown from around 20 attending in the 1960's to more than 1,000 today. Eleanor and I were greatly honored on our visit to Hebron for the 1992 conference, where a crowd of more than 1,200 tribal Christians welcomed us. I believe we shook every hand! After a special meeting in the pavilion, the tribal leaders led us to another part of the property. To our amazement, they had built a special Bible Training Center, dedicated in our honor. The cornerstone reads:

Rev. & Mrs. D.J. Walsh
Training Center
6th December 1992

Through my tears, I couldn't resist pointing out to the celebrating crowd that the new training center faces the exact spot on the Matamahari River bank where Eleanor and I lived with our children in 1960.

Reliving the past 35 years, we have seen God's mighty hand at work among the tribal people of Bangladesh. The odds that Eleanor and I faced when we embarked on our missionary journey were daunting. BUT GOD . . .!

We, and others of our missionary colleagues, spent the best years of our lives struggling often against the attacks of the great enemy, Satan. Paul Miller and Harry Goehring sacrificed their lives. Nationals like Ancherai, Robichandro, Gonachandro, and Gunijon have traversed the Chittagong Hill Tracts in tireless efforts to reach their people for Christ. Has this been in vain? Never! The apostle John, while exiled in prison on the Island of Patmos, had the privilege of seeing that for which we all have toiled during our short lifetime in Bangladesh. He said,

"After this I beheld, and, lo, a great multitude which no man could number, of all nations, and kindreds, and people, and tongues, stood before the throne, and before the Lamb, clothed with white robes, and palms in their hands; And cried with a loud voice, saying, Salvation to our God which sitteth upon the throne, and unto the Lamb" (Revelation 7: 9–10.)

Eleanor and I have had the wonderful privilege of living and working with the tribal people of Bangladesh. The day will come when we, like the apostle John, will spend eternity with the believers glorifying the Lamb of God, before the throne.

To Him be all the glory!

Nepal
Bhutan
Darjeeling
ASSAM INDIA
Bogra
Mymensingh
BANGLADESH
Dhaka
INDIA
Comilla
Calcutta
Chittagong Hill Tracts Jungle
Chittagong
Hebron
Cheringa
Cox's Bazar
BURMA
Bay of Bengal
Akyab

INDIA
Indian
Ocean
Bay of
Bengal

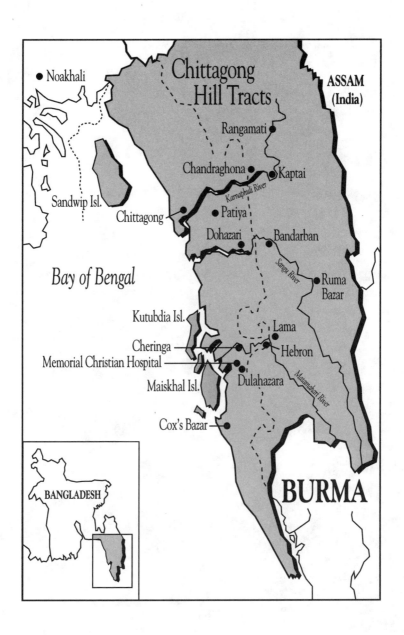

Noakhali

Chittagong
Hill Tracts

ASSAM
(India)

Rangamati

Chandraghona   Kaptai

Sandwip Isl.   *Karnaphuli River*

Chittagong   Patiya

Dohazari   Bandarban

Bay of Bengal   *Sangu River*

Ruma
Bazar

Kutubdia Isl.

Lama

Cheringa   Hebron

Memorial Christian Hospital

Maiskhal Isl.   Dulahazara   *Matamohari River*

Cox's Bazar

BURMA

BANGLADESH